Supporting science, design and technology in the early years

Supporting early learning

Series Editors: Vicky Hurst and Jenefer Joseph

The focus of this series is on improving the effectiveness of early education. Policy developments come and go, and difficult decisions are often forced on those with responsibility for young children's well-being. This series aims to help with these decisions by showing how developmental approaches to early education provide a sound and positive basis for learning.

Each book recognizes that children from birth to six years old have particular developmental needs. This applies just as much to the acquisition of subject knowledge, skills and understanding as to other educational goals such as social skills, attitudes and dispositions. The importance of providing a learning environment which is carefully planned to stimulate children's own active learning is also stressed.

Throughout the series, readers are encouraged to reflect on the education being offered to young children, through revisiting developmental principles and using them to analyse their observations of children. In this way, readers can evaluate ideas about the most effective ways of educating young children and develop strategies for approaching their practice in ways which offer every child a more appropriate education.

Published titles:

Bernadette Duffy: *Supporting Creativity and Imagination in the Early Years*
Vicky Hurst and Jenefer Joseph: *Supporting Early Learning: The Way Forward*
Linda Pound: *Supporting Mathematical Development in the Early Years*
John Siraj-Blatchford and Iain MacLeod-Brudenell: *Supporting Science, Design and Technology in the Early Years*
Marian Whitehead: *Supporting Language and Literacy Development in the Early Years*

● ● ● Supporting science, design and technology in the early years

John Siraj-Blatchford
Iain MacLeod-Brudenell

Open University Press
Maidenhead · Philadelphia

Open University Press
McGraw-Hill House
Shoppenhangers Road
Maidenhead
Berkshire
England
SL6 2QL

email: enquiries@openup.co.uk
world wide web : http://www.openup.co.uk

and

325 Chestnut Street
Philadelphia, PA 19106, USA

First Published 1999
Reprinted 2003

A catalogue record of this book is available from the British Library

ISBN   0 335 19942 9 (pb)   0 335 19943 7 (hb)

Library of Congress Cataloging-in-Publication Data
Siraj-Blatchford, John, 1952–
    Supporting science, design and technology in the early years/
John Siraj-Blatchford and Iain McLeod Brudenell.
        p. cm. – (Supporting early learning)
    Includes bibliographical references and index.
    ISBN 0-335-19943-7. – ISBN 0-335-19942-9 (pbk.)
    1. Technology – Study and teaching (Early childhood) 2. Science – Study
and teaching (Early childhood) I. MacLeod-Brudenell, Iain. II. Title.
III. Series.
T65.3.S55   1999
372.3'5–dc21   98–47062
                                                                           CIP

Typeset by Type Study, Scarborough
Printed in Great Britain by Biddles Ltd, www.biddles.co.uk

Contents

List of boxes

List of figures and table

Acknowledgements

We wish to thank all of the children, parents and early childhood staff that have contributed to this book and to our understanding of all the issues with which it is concerned. We must also thank our students for their contributions. We have both been extremely fortunate in having the opportunity to work with a great many talented educators in a wide range of early childhood settings.

We owe a special debt of gratitude to our series editors, to Jenefer and to Vicky, who was so tragically taken from us before she had the opportunity to see the final manuscript.

We would also like to thank Shona Mullen at Open University Press for her valuable advice and for her patience; we must also thank our families: Iram and Jo, Dorcas, Candida, Rory and Patrick for putting up with us all those times we were occupied with the writing when we should have been paying greater attention to them.

Series editors' preface

This book is one of a series which will be of interest to all those concerned with the care and education of children from birth to 6 years old – child-minders, teachers and other professionals in schools, those who work in playgroups, private and community nurseries and similar institutions; governors, providers and managers. We also speak to parents and carers, whose involvement is probably the most influential of all for children's learning and development.

Our focus is on improving the effectiveness of early education. Policy developments come and go, and difficult decisions are often forced on all those with responsibility for young children's well-being. We aim to help with these decisions by showing how developmental approaches to young children's education not only accord with our fundamental educational principles, but provide a positive and sound basis for learning.

Each book recognizes and demonstrates that children from birth to 6 years old have particular developmental learning needs, and that all those providing care and education for them would be wise to approach their work developmentally. This applies just as much to the acquisition of subject knowledge, skills and understanding, as to other educational goals such as social skills, attitudes and dispositions. In this series there are several volumes with a subject-based focus, and the main aim is to show how that can be introduced to young children within the framework of an integrated and developmentally appropriate curriculum, without losing its integrity as an area of knowledge in its own right. We also stress the importance of providing a learning environment which is carefully planned for children's own active learning. The present volume helps to dispel the anxieties which many practitioners have about their own expertise in, and understanding of science, design and technology. It will help to stimulate adults' enthusiasm for these vital areas of learning, and offers many examples of practical ways of initiating young children into them.

Access for all children is fundamental to the provision of educational opportunity. We are concerned to emphasize anti-discriminatory approaches throughout, as well as the importance of recognizing that meeting special educational needs must be an integral purpose of curriculum development and planning. We see the role of play in learning as a central one, and one which also relates to all-round emotional, social and physical development. Play, along with other forms of active learning, is normally a natural point of access to the curriculum for each child at his or her particular stage and level of understanding. It is therefore an essential force in making for equal opportunities in learning, intrinsic as it is to all areas of development. We believe that these two aspects, play and equal opportunities, are so important that we not only highlight them in each volume in this series, but also include separate volumes on them as well.

Throughout this series, we encourage readers to reflect on the education being offered to young children, through revisiting the developmental principles which most practitioners hold, and using them to analyse their observations of the children. In this way, readers can evaluate ideas about the most effective ways of educating young children, and develop strategies for approaching their practice in ways which exemplify their fundamental educational beliefs, and offer every child a more appropriate education.

The authors of each book in the series subscribe to the following set of principles for a developmental curriculum:

Principles for a developmental curriculum

- Each child is an individual and should be respected and treated as such.
- The early years are a period of development in their own right, and education of young children should be seen as a specialism with its own valid criteria of appropriate practice.
- The role of the educator of young children is to engage actively with what most concerns the child, and to support learning through these preoccupations.
- The educator has a responsibility to foster positive attitudes in children to both self and others, and to counter negative messages which children may have received.

- Each child's cultural and linguistic endowment is seen as the fundamental medium of learning.
- An anti-discriminatory approach is the basis of all respect-worthy education, and is essential as a criterion for a developmentally appropriate curriculum (DAC).
- All children should be offered equal opportunities to progress and develop, and should have equal access to good quality provision. The concepts of multiculturalism and anti-racism are intrinsic to this whole educational approach.
- Partnership with parents should be given priority as the most effective means of ensuring coherence and continuity in children's experiences, and in the curriculum offered to them.
- A democratic perspective permeates education of good quality and is the basis of transactions between people.

Vicky Hurst and Jenefer Joseph

Introduction

The first time we saw Patrick was on the photo of the scan . . . the next time was when he arrived – seven weeks early (Fran had to have an emergency Caesarean). He seemed healthy and didn't need to go in an incubator but after a few days at home he was back in hospital for an operation. He was constantly monitored by a computer – which was operated by touching the screen.

Within the first few weeks of his life Patrick had experienced many forms of technology. Even before his birth his parents and grandparents had been able to see him as a result of a technological process. Our interactions with technology and science are both profound and lifelong. Every part of life is affected by the results of scientific investigation and the products of technology. Our earliest sensory experiences involve touching, tasting, smelling, listening to, or looking at the products of scientific and technological activity. Our natural inclinations to explore and to try things out play a profound role in our early learning. Food technologies are immediately significant to the very young child; they eat processed food products and food that is cooked at home. It may even be prepared in a food processor or microwave oven. As parents we act as food technologists, we adapt and combine food products to suit our children's tastes. Proportions are often systematically varied and tested. Experiments are conducted. When we place a mobile above a baby's cot the stimulus that we are offering triggers off a conscious process of interaction with technology that will develop throughout the child's life.

Before long children begin to play with toys which may have moving parts and mechanisms; these toys will be made of a variety of materials including plastic or fabric or wood. They begin to learn about the properties that these materials possess: Are they soft and smooth? Are they flexible? Are they strong? Even when children are sleeping they will experience and be influenced by the technological products around them: their cot, their mattress, their quilt. Many parents have been concerned to read scientific reports that relate the risk of cot death syndrome to various qualities of these commercial products.

Once consideration is made of the impact of science and technology on our lives, and with the everyday as well as the extraordinary uses we make of technology, it becomes evident that all people are the beneficiaries of science and technology. We are all users of technology but this is not in a purely passive way. When we choose a toothbrush we consider its design features; we have evaluated the one that we have been using; considered how well it fits the hand and the mouth; the hardness of the bristles, the size of the toothbrush head. We evaluate the feel, the handling qualities and effectiveness of it as a *product* and of its usefulness in *application*. Things like toothbrushes are made, the products of someone's technical skill in designing and making and they are evaluated, used, explored through each of our senses.

We all use science and technology and we are all practising scientists and technologists as well. We all try to provide explanations for things that we experience, we measure things at times and we try things out. However modestly, from time to time, we also design or adapt and make things, whether these are food products, the occasional item of clothing or a bookshelf. We may design and construct a new layout for our garden, and we are even more often responsible for the interior decoration, layout and choice of furniture in our homes. If we are to encourage young children to grow up to be good at these things we must start by trying to see the world through their eyes and support them in their own inquiries and projects. Increasingly we can broaden their horizons and show them that with our support there is so much more that they can achieve, and that they can look forward to achieving independently in the future.

This book provides a novel approach to supporting young children's learning in science and design and technology. We know that the approach is effective from our own experience but the general approach may be unfamiliar to some of our readers. For this reason some theoretical explanations are necessary. In the interests of avoiding interruptions in what we consider to be an essentially practical text, many extended explanations have been restricted to appendixes. However, some broad introductory comments *are* necessary and it is to these that we now turn.

Design and technology: encouraging children to make things

The broad aims and provisions for teaching design and technology in the UK were defined for the first time in the National Curriculum; the subject was devised with an emphasis upon the development of children's practical *capability*. Children therefore *design, make* and *evaluate* their own products in primary school classrooms throughout the country. The areas of knowledge and experience that are outlined in the curriculum documents cover the use of food and textiles, construction kits, making things from wood and other construction materials and communicating ideas through the use of drawings and other media. These are areas of experience that are familiar, for the most part, to those working with young children. In fact, as far as the early years curriculum is concerned, we might consider the foundations of these design and technology educational practices to have been set over a period of two centuries by the pioneers of the kindergarten and nursery education movement.

Comenius, in the seventeenth century, and Pestalozzi, Froebel, and Owen in the nineteenth century all extolled the virtues of young children being industrious. They encouraged educators to provide opportunities for infants to make things. Froebel's proposals, as far back as 1829, included the suggestion that children should spend each afternoon in crafts that included the making of wooden kitchen utensils, weaving, the use of pasteboard to make stars, wheels, boxes, napkin rings and lamp shades. He also suggested that children might be encouraged to whittle boats, windmills and water wheels, and that they should model with clay and flexible wire. For Froebel, education in manual skills served to develop the whole child; his concern was much more than merely vocational. Froebel believed that craft provided a means of expression and a powerful means to develop habits of thought that included: 'success, a calm sense of power, a firm conviction of mastership, which are so essential to fullness of life' (Frobel 1887: 37).

In different ways, Maria Montessori, Jean Piaget and John Dewey all took this emphasis upon craft even further and also argued that classification, and the power to distinguish between qualities and attributes, actually provided the foundations of intelligence: 'To be able to distinguish, classify and catalogue external things on the basis of a secure order already established in the mind, this is at once intelligence and culture' (Montessori 1912: 205). As we shall see, sorting and classification play a major part in science education, and they also have a major role to play in design and technology. In integrating design education with the craft tradition, design and technology educators placed a new emphasis upon the 'evaluation' of technological products. The implications of this will be explained more fully in the next chapter. For the time being it is enough to note that this provides a part of our justification for adopting an integrated approach to supporting science, design and technology.

The integrated approach to science and design and technology education

Evaluation plays a part in both science and design and technology. We have found that it is often appropriate to subject the products of both children's and adults' design and technology to forms of scientific evaluation. Scientific investigations and explanations also provide the stimulus for many designing and making activities. Many adults found their own science education alienating and this provided us with yet another reason for adopting the integrated approach. In providing guidance and illustrations of good practice in science education we have made every effort to ensure that the relevance is clear. As Hurst and Joseph (1998: 14) put it: 'Children learn best in social contexts, when they are interacting in meaningful ways with their peers or with adults'.

Design and technology often provide the most relevant social contexts for understanding science. The integrated approach is also consistent with the School Curriculum and Assessment Authority (SCAA) *Desirable Outcomes for Children's Learning* (1996) that are discussed in depth in Chapter 5. Perhaps even more importantly, the integrated approach that we have taken is consistent with an academic tradition that in recent years has been having an influence on all sectors of education. As a curriculum subject, science, technology and society (STS) has sought to introduce an approach to science education that emphasizes a study of the nature of science and technology and of the social effects of technological change. In a survey identifying the opinions of their members regarding the direction of future developments within science education, the Association for Science Education (ASE) has also found that most teachers now feel that the subject should be set within a more holistic curriculum framework that emphasizes 'relevance' (ASE 1998). It may be that in future years we will therefore see greater integration throughout the school curriculum.

Science education in the early years

We often talk of children as 'natural scientists' (Bentley and Watts 1994), and of their natural inclination to 'spontaneously wonder' (Donaldson 1992) about things:

From the very earliest days in its life, a child develops beliefs about the things that happen in its surroundings. The baby lets go of the rattle and it falls to the ground; it does it again and the pattern repeats itself. It pushes a ball and it goes on rolling across the floor. In this way, sets of expectations are established which enable the child to begin to make predictions. Initially these are isolated and independent of one another. However, as the child grows older, all its experiences of pushing, pulling, lifting, throwing and feeling and seeing things stimulate the development of more generalised sets of expectations and the ability to make predictions about a wider range of experiences. By the time the child receives formal teaching in science it has already constructed a set of beliefs about a wide range of natural phenomena.

(Driver 1985: 2)

As Driver (1985) goes on to suggest, we now know that some of the beliefs that children develop turn out to differ markedly from accepted scientific knowledge and that young children's views are often difficult to change. This has important consequences for science educational approaches that are based on the notion of children finding things out for themselves, for 'discovery' learning. Left entirely to their own devices, children will learn about the world around them, but the trouble is they will often learn to understand it in idiosyncratic (and less useful) ways. A few very common examples may illustrate the point:

- Children often consider that a vacuum 'sucks', yet a 'vacuum', that is by definition 'nothing' can clearly be *doing* nothing;
- When children put their hands in cold water or stand barefoot on a tiled floor they will refer to the cold coming 'into' them rather than to the heat escaping from them;
- Children believe that heavy things fall faster;
- They believe that things float simply because they are 'light';
- They fail to recognize that they can see because light is reflected from the things around them and that this enters their eyes, they imagine something comes *from* their eyes to sense the things around them.

It may be many years later, in adolescence or adulthood, that we come across a better scientific explanation for these things. Many adults never come across them.

The scientific beliefs that individual children build up on their own and the science that is constructed by professional scientists is qualitatively different. When we accept the scientific knowledge that is produced by professional scientists we do so because we know that the ideas have been communicated throughout the scientific community and they have been subjected to rigorous testing. 'Established' scientific knowledge is the product of a collective and collaborative historical enterprise. When we refer to science as a 'discipline' we also draw attention to the fact that it constitutes an intellectual enterprise that has a distinct set of rules and that these rules are normally (or properly) adhered to by that particular academic community we know as 'scientists'. For a child (or for anyone else) to think 'scientifically' means to obey these rules, to keep an open mind, to respect yet always to critically evaluate evidence, and to participate in a community that encourages the free exchange of information, critical peer review and testing. This latter point is crucial because, as Driver *et al.* (1996: 44) have put it: 'Scientific knowledge is the product of a community, not of an individual. Findings reported by an individual must survive an institutional checking and testing mechanism, before being accepted as knowledge'.

All of this can be carried out to good effect in infant classrooms and preschool settings. The National Curriculum for science in primary schools has been developed to teach children some of the key ideas at the same time as developing their investigative skills. The central task of a science education is therefore to give children an appreciation of the historical accomplishments of the scientific community and an introduction to the scientific practices that provide the means by which they are achieved. In the early years this is best achieved by providing young children with practical 'hands-on' experiences, and drawing their attention to some of the scientific theories that are available to explain these experiences. It is also achieved by answering their questions and telling them stories about significant developments and discoveries. To do this well, we need to build up our repertoire of appropriate stories and develop our knowledge of everyday phenomena. Science provides us with explanations for a broad range of phenomena that is of interest to young children: Why is the sky blue? What happens to the tadpoles? How does a torch work? Where does all of the water go to after it goes down to the sea? Science also provides the means by which predictions can be made: What will happen when you mix vinegar and baking powder together? What happens when you squash a plastic bottle full of air under water? What will the moon look like tomorrow night?[1]

In addition to passing on the best explanations available we also need to help children understand how it was that these ideas came to be discovered. The best way of doing this is to carry out some investigations with the children ourselves. As Black (1993: 10) put it, in his general discussion of primary school science learning programmes: 'A first essential is that students should come to understand science and to understand how science is made by being engaged in doing it'. As we shall see, this book takes the view that this work can also be developed in any home, nursery or other preschool setting and that it is most usefully presented to young children as 'playing the scientist game'.

Playing the scientist game

It has often been assumed that the central aim of science education is to teach children as much as possible about what scientists have learnt. A similar view could be taken in design and technology where the subject would then be limited to teaching children about the products of influential schools of design, and about particular techniques and technologies. While all of these certainly have a place in science and design and technology education it is now widely agreed that the central focus of both subjects should be on the development of practical capability. Children should therefore be systematically introduced to the 'craft skills' of the scientist and those of the design technologist.

Children should therefore be introduced to these particular ways of working and thinking and apply them to their own investigations and problems at an early stage. Just as portrait or landscape painters need to learn techniques and technicalities to practise their art effectively, and just as they will benefit from studying the paintings of others, so the scientist and the design technologist gain from similarly focused tuition in their own fields. The point is that these focused activities are not the ends in themselves, they are merely the means by which children are given their first appreciation and are later more formally introduced to each of these 'craft' communities. As Robin Millar (1989: 60) has suggested:

> In teaching children science, we are helping them to internalise the procedures and standards of the scientific community. We are assisting the child to construct for herself a mental representation of the scientific ways of working and judging.

Millar (1989: 60) cites Lawrence Stenhouse (1978) to argue for a model of teaching in which 'the teacher guides the learner towards an appreciation of the standards of judgment inherent in a discipline, through a process of day-to-day correction and critical comment on the learner's work'.

The most important personal skill for a scientist is the skill of reasoning. More accurately, it is the skill of identifying mistaken reasoning. We can all reason incorrectly easily enough. Aristotle thought that a heavier object would fall to the ground faster than a light one. It won't, but the fact that he got it wrong doesn't mean that he was stupid – far from it. Aristotle would have been quick to correct himself if he had carried out a systematic study. Galileo is often credited as being the first to make the necessary measurements, but it is important to recognize that that was all that it took. Galileo may or may not have been the first to make the measurements, but his spectacular demonstration on the leaning tower of Pisa certainly popularized the idea. It made history! Let's take a more mundane example from a school PE lesson involving 4 and 5-year-olds:

> To the tune of 'The Sorcerer's Apprentice' the group of infants were jumping, feet together, around the school hall imitating 'magical brushes' that were sweeping away the water. As the children began to tire one child, Sarah, suddenly exclaimed; 'It's not fair Brahmajit can jump further because he has longer legs!' The teacher stopped the class and repeated what Sarah had said. She then lined the children up in order of their height. Each in turn was asked to jump and the children were invited to judge which children jumped farthest. It certainly looked as though Sarah's hypothesis was correct. The teacher had encouraged the children to make systematic observations, to organize the observations into an orderly array so that any pattern would be easier to see. However misleading the evidence here, the teacher was demonstrating some rigorous scientific reasoning. She could have left it at that but she had doubts and decided to persevere to test the hypothesis further, and this demonstrated her real commitment to science education. On the way back to the classroom, she took two of the children into the library and showed them where the books on sport were located; she asked them to collect together all the picture of famous athletes they could find.
>
> When the children were dressed they sat on the carpet in front of the teacher and were invited to look closely at the pictures in the books. Which athletes were the jumpers? Which athletes had the longest legs? Again the evidence seemed to show that Sarah's hypothesis was correct. The teacher suggested that the children should test the hypothesis further and asked the children how they might each measure the length of their legs and the distance they could jump. The teacher emphasized the fact that everyone would have to measure their legs and jumps in the same way or the test would not be 'fair'. The methods were agreed and over the following week the children, in pairs, measured their legs. A sheet of sugar paper was first pinned to the wall and each took their turn in drawing around each other's right leg. They then cut out the silhouette of their leg and wrote their name upon it. The teacher supervised the arrangement of the legs on a wall display. By the end of the week the lower part of the wall was covered

with the leg silhouettes. They were arranged in order of height and just before the children went into the hall for their PE lesson the teacher asked them how they thought they would be arranged if each were put in order of distance they could jump. The children agreed that, if the hypothesis was correct, the legs would be in the same order. The teacher pinned a thread across the tops of the legs to show the gradual curve upwards.

In the hall the children chalked lines, jumped and counted the decimetre divisions on their meter measuring sticks. One child complained that his partner was cheating because he put his toe instead of his heel on the line. Again the teacher stopped all of the children to discuss how they might be sure to make the test fair. After a few minutes each paper 'leg' had a number written on it and the teacher lined the children up according to the number and length of their jump before returning to the classroom. Still in order the children lined up against the wall and pinned their leg in its place. When they stood back they could see that the gradual incline had given way to unevenness and that the pattern was gone. The children concluded that the hypothesis was wrong. So why were some of the children able to jump further than others? One of the suggestions was that some children had stronger legs and the teacher therefore arranged some bathroom scales against a wall so that the children could measure the strength of their 'leg pushes' over the following week.

When the teacher decided to continue to test the generalization that had been made (that longer legs meant longer jumps) she was demonstrating to the children a fundamental principle of the scientific enterprise. She was demonstrating that no generalization should be allowed to stand unless it is repeatedly tested by newer and newer experiments and more and more accurate forms of measurement. While Sarah may have been a little disappointed that her hypothesis was ultimately proved incorrect, it had become the property of the whole class before it was found wanting. The children did not, in fact, seem disappointed at all, but were rather excited to find themselves testing yet another hypothesis (prediction) that they had identified so soon.

To take another example, this time drawn from a professional development package produced at the Manchester Metropolitan University (Abbott *et al.* 1996), a younger group of nursery children were playing the scientist game in the context of a 'ladybird hunt'.[2] A number of the activities within the nursery had been centred around the topic of living things and patterns in nature so that when one of the children had said they had seen a ladybird in a raised flower bed this was seen as an excellent opportunity. Before the first group of children embarked upon the lady-bird hunt, a member of the nursery staff spent a few minutes showing them some of the centre's reference books that featured ladybirds. As she talked to the children she seemed genuinely curious about the insects and this encouraged the children to take an interest too. They looked at the pic-tures and talked about the spots and the wings and the wing covers. They also talked about how they should always take care of living things. There was an air of anticipation and excitement before they embarked outside. The video then shows the children inspecting the foliage in the flower beds and hedgerows and then returning with some specimens to the centre. In the preliminary discussions, outside on the hunt, and back in the centre a lot of questions were asked:

> What colours are they?
> How many spots do they have?
> Are they hiding?
> Where shall we find them?
> What do they eat?
> What does it feel like?
> Will it fly away?
> How many legs has it got?
> What shape is its body?

The children looked at the ladybirds through their magnifying glasses. They counted their spots with the help of the adult and they allowed them to crawl across their hands, and watched them fly. The children were then given the opportunity to make their own model ladybirds out of red and black playdough. This activity was chosen specifically to encourage the children's visual perception. The video then shows how the children returned to the hunt quite spontaneously in their free play and were clearly very much engaged in the topic for some time afterwards.

In both of the above cases, the investigative processes that were fol-lowed by the teacher can be represented in a simple diagrammatic form that has been found helpful in planning. The same approach is employed to support teachers in developing design and technology activities. The planning diagrams are provided in Chapter 4. The major difference between the two investigations cited above was in the degree of support and role modelling provided by the educator. In the first case the teacher was able to develop the investigation in collaboration with the children. In the latter case there was a need to provide more support and to demon-strate by their own actions and discussion what it was to look at things sci-entifically. All of the investigations and designing and making activities that we provide need to be matched to the children's capabilities in this way and Chapters 5 and 6 will therefore focus on the curriculum, resourcing, assessment, progression and continuity. Before we go on to these areas of concern for curriculum planning and development an effort will be made to show how science and design and technology education relate to the broader concerns of teaching and learning in early childhood. Chapter 1 will begin by developing many of the ideas introduced in this chapter. It will be argued that a good deal of both science and design and technology education should build upon existing practice. Chapter 2 is concerned with developing practices that are responsive to the differing needs of children. Issues relate to culture, gender, bilingualism, physical difference and the children's differing emotional needs. In Chapter 3 the literature on early childhood play and development will be reviewed to identify the role to be played by adults in supporting the child's scientific and design and technological development.

Notes

1 If you feel at all unsure about the answers to any of the questions that are referred to on this page or at any other point in the book, you shouldn't be in any way concerned about it. When we started to teach science we didn't know how to explain many of these things either. We believe it was the quality of our own science education that needed to be questioned. Suitable explanations are provided in Appendix 1, and Appendix 2 provides a range of other reference sources that you may find useful in dealing with children's questions.
2 The activity is included as a video case study in the resource pack which includes a number of other useful studies related to the six key areas of the School Curriculum and Assessment Authority (SCAA) *Desirable Outcomes for Children's Learning on Starting Compulsory Schooling* (SCAA 1996).

Science, design and technology in the home and local environment

It is not always easy to show the degree of interest and patience that I would like when, in the middle of making three packed lunches before the 8.30 a.m. school deadline, my six year old daughter asks, 'Why have my cornflakes gone all soggy?' In this case I know that I handled the situation badly. Basically I ignored her for as long as I could, before trying to 'fob' her off with an explanation that was way 'above her head', because I didn't take the time to assess her level of understanding. When she persisted, I tried, unsuccessfully, to divert her interest towards the 'send away for a free toy' information on the side of the packet. Eventually, flustered and frustrated, I resorted to an example of what I might sarcastically call the ultimate in 'positive parenting', the domineering stance, the wagging finger and the words; 'Well, if you hadn't spent fifteen minutes messing around in your bedroom, they wouldn't be all soggy now would they?

(Webster 1997: 1)

It is often difficult to support our children's curiosity and their knowledge and understanding of science. In the above account Leigh Webster, a mature teacher education student, and a science specialist, identifies some of the problems graphically. Leigh, like many parents, tries to give her children as full an answer to their questions as she is able, but on this occasion she responded negatively because she was too busy to deal with the child's question at that time. This sometimes happens to us all and we shouldn't feel guilty about it. Let's face it, the child does learn something on these occasions, if only to be more considerate when their parent is busy. Ideally we remember the question and can return to it later; 'Do you remember darling, your question about the cornflakes? Well I was thinking about it – shall we see what happens when we put just one little drop of milk at a time on a cornflake to see if we can figure it out?' The child would then see how the flake gradually swelled up as the liquid is slowly absorbed. They would also see how an experiment is conducted and that their parent shared and supported their curiosity and exploration.

Another common problem is when we fail to communicate effectively with the child. Margaret Donaldson (1992: 44) includes the following interaction in her book *Human Minds* that illustrates the phenomenon very well. It involves a child aged 3 years and 11 months who was standing with an adult in a country lane. The child 'spontaneously wonders' about a car that is observed parked on a concrete drive outside a house:

Jamie: Why is it [*the car*] on that metal thing?
Adult: It's not metal, it's concrete.
Jamie: Why is it on the concrete thing?
Adult: Well, when it rains the ground gets soft and muddy, doesn't it?
  [*Jamie nods, bends down and scratches the dry earth.*]
Adult: So the wheels would sink into the mud. But the concrete's hard, you see.
Jamie [excitedly]: But the concrete's soft in the mix! Why is it soft in the mix?

Donaldson tells us that the adult was thrown into confusion at this point and was unable to answer Jamie's question which suggests (unsurprisingly) that the adult didn't immediately think of the 'mix' of the concrete. In retrospect it might have been obvious that Jamie had seen a concrete mixer or some concrete being mixed by hand before. In any event, one can imagine Jamie having seen the soft and wet substance being mixed and an obliging adult had informed him at that time that the substance was called 'concrete'. When he was subsequently told concrete was hard and dry, he needed some explanation; and he was ready to learn that some substances can be found in both liquid and solid states. This is an important scientific concept that is included in the National Curriculum. The adult's unfortunate failure to engage with the child really does represent a missed opportunity. We have to accept though that these opportunities are not always easy to identify.

Donaldson refers to another interaction, between a child 'around four years of age', and her mother. The case also shows how important it is to judge the child's mood, or mode of thinking. The couple are travelling on a bus:

> *Child:*   Mum, where's the moon? Why is it not there tonight?
>   [*The sky was dark, no moon was visible.*]
> *Mother:* The moon's gone to its bed.
> *Child* [indignantly]: Moons don't have beds!

Apparently this was too much for the mother; after a few seconds of silence she said helplessly: 'Well where *do* they sleep then?' Then she changed the subject. The child was thinking scientifically, but at another time she might easily have been amused by the image of the moon in bed. The point that we are trying to make here might be more easily understood if we reverse the roles. If we imagine the child suggesting that the moon has 'gone to bed' a scientific explanation from the parent would be entirely inappropriate. The child should not be given an appreciation of science at the *expense* of other ways of looking at the world. We need to be alert for those occasions when the child is being poetic or engaging in fantasy, and support those ways of thinking too. The trick is to adopt a balanced approach and to encourage and support both.

Seeing things through the child's eyes

Young children learn from everything that happens to them. They don't separate their learning into subjects and although this book focuses on science and design and technology children experience these areas of learning set within a much wider context. There are many ways of helping a child to build on the foundation of natural curiosity, the urge to explore, to investigate, to try things out to see what happens.

Adults provide crucial role models for young children. In order that we may effectively help them we therefore need to be explorers with our children. We need to show them that we can learn alongside them and that we can share in the pleasures of learning in science and design and technology. We must actively involve ourselves in wondering and remember that scientific and technological thinking is part of our everyday experience. It is not, and has never been, something done exclusively by men in white coats and we don't have to imagine ourselves in that role to support children. It is rather a way of questioning and responding to our everyday experience.

So how *do* children see things? To begin with we should remind ourselves that as adults we see things from a different perspective – not only from a physically different perspective but also from a perspective developed from greater experience. From a child's height things take on a different slant. It is worth making the effort to imagine how things appear from the height of a small child. Some objects can be seen more clearly, for example door handles, shelf brackets and table legs, while other things such as light switches, lamp bulbs and window fasteners are less easily visible. If we focus our attention on those mechanisms that are easily visible and accessible we will therefore be looking at things that are more immediately relevant to the child. If we explain to young children how such things work we will be encouraging a developing understanding of concepts relating to functional dependency, forces and technological systems.

It is a lot more difficult to look at things with the freshness of approach that children bring to new experiences. It may well be that as adults we have a good deal to gain from looking at things through the child's eyes in this sense. A series of very interesting experiments were conducted for the Children's Learning in Science (CLIS) project at Leeds University (Brooks and Driver 1989). One experiment involved children aged, 5, 8, 12 and 16. Two inflated balloons were hung at either end of a balance. The children were asked; 'If we let air out of one of the balloons, which way will the other one move?' The correct answer was 'down' because the air in the balloon has weight that is being released. The results of this test, and a range of other similar ones as well, showed that all of the 5-year-olds gave the right answer, and so did three out of four of the 8-year-olds, but none of the 12-year-olds and only one in three of the 16-year-olds were able to provide the correct answer. What this experiment probably illustrates is the way in which new experiences sometimes cause our ideas to be modified. Unfortunately many of these modifications are liable to produce misconceptions that may be quite difficult to shake off. This is a process referred to earlier and it has been widely researched. Driver (1985: 26) discusses the process:

> The ways that younger children explain and interpret certain natural events were explored by Jean Piaget in his well known early works in which he asked children such questions as, 'What causes night?', 'How do clouds move?' and 'Which of these objects is alive?' These studies have been extensively replicated and the results are still worth scrutiny in terms of the ideas children of different ages suggest. One might ask, for example, what implication it might have for introductory Biology courses if one takes seriously the finding that over 10 per cent of 11-year-olds in Britain extend their concept of 'living things' to include the sun, wind and fire.

We don't yet know why it is that the 12-year-olds got the question about the balloons wrong. Hopefully some enterprising researcher will be able to give us the answer in the future. It may even be that Bruner (1966) is correct in arguing that: 'much of what we do and say in school only makes children feel that they don't know things that in fact they know perfectly well before we began to talk to them.' It may be the additional knowledge that they have acquired over the years that is causing them confusion. They may have been thinking about a vacuum, or about balloons filled with a gas such as helium that is lighter than air. Whatever the reason, the implications are that we should be more concerned with giving children understanding than teaching them 'facts' and we need to help children to relate new knowledge to what they already know in a meaningful way.

Box 1.1 Learning science when washing up

Waseem (a 3-year-old) stands on the chair at the sink to wash some of his toys; he plunges his plastic teapot into the bubble-filled water. The teapot fills with water and bubbles come out of the spout. He says, 'The teapot, it's blowing bubbles!' A plastic ball floats on the surface and no matter how hard he pushes it, it always returns to the surface. 'The ball keeps jumping out of the water', he says. He decides it must be the water pushing it up. This is 'upthrust' (see Appendix 1).

Children observe and we must observe children

'Observation' is commonly discussed as a key scientific skill, but it would be a mistake to imagine that observations are simply collected over time and lead to our developing more and more complete understandings as we get older. Unless we encourage them to do otherwise, as children get older they increasingly simplify their understandings of the world. As Johnston (1996: 31) put it, they 'filter out' all of those things that they believe to be unimportant, 'because the world becomes too large for them to observe everything'.

As Johnston suggests, the scientist needs to focus on those observations most relevant to the investigation, they need to focus in, but they also need to be able to make broad observations before they begin to focus on these . specific observations. In fact young children do a great deal of observing; they avidly watch all kinds of activities. As previously suggested we can also encourage them to observe more by acting as good role models and exploring new ideas and experiences with them. Social learning theorists such as Albert Bandura have shown that children learn a great deal from observing and imitating others. The child does not simply imitate everyone else they observe, however, the behaviour of some peers and adults is considered more important to the child than others. They model aspects of their own behaviour on these 'significant others'. According to Bandura children tend to model their behaviour on others who are warm and loving towards them, those who seem to have more power, influence and competence, and those seen as similar to themselves (of the same age, sex etc).

Bandura claims that most of what children learn is the result of observation and modelling. The reasons for this are as follows:

1 Learning by observing someone else achieve a good result is a lot more efficient than learning by trial and error, or waiting until a reinforcement is given.

2 Many abilities that children master could probably not be learned by simple trial and error. Learning to use a language is probably the best example. Listening to someone, and then incorporating their words or grammar into correct speech is largely the result of observational learning.

(Davenport 1994: 110)

Young children observe all kinds of things and sometimes they have a specific scientific or technological connection. Increasingly we can draw their attention to the relevant scientific and technological features demonstrated by the things that they observe. They may be watching people walking in the rain, digging the garden, or programming a video recorder. They may ask questions about it or they may join in. At such times we can say that children are 'involved', no matter how passively, in the activity. Laevers (1993), defines such involvement as a quality of human activity which usually:

- can be recognised by a child's concentration and persistence;
- is characterised by motivation, fascination, an openness to stimuli and an intensity of experience both at the physical and cognitive level, and a deep satisfaction with a strong flow of energy;
- is determined by the 'exploratory' drive and the child's individual developmental needs;
- as a result of involvement there is evidence to suggest that development occurs.

To fully capitalize on the child's involvement it is necessary to be aware of the central role of engaging (especially talking) with the children. The importance of quality conversation cannot be overemphasized, and we are therefore indebted to Wynn Harlen and Paul Black for introducing us to the notion of 'talk cycle'. The rules are simple, observe the child and then either begin a conversation or respond to his or her remarks:

The talk cycle
- listen to the child – take what she or he says seriously;
- try to understand what they mean;
- use the child's meaning as the basis for the next adult comment, remark, suggestion, or question;
- try to speak or act in a way that the child understands.

What is good practice within the home is also good practice in play-groups, nurseries and schools. We need to recognize, however, that if we are to help children to develop at their own pace but with support, we need to provide them with the intellectual tools that they need to make sense of their world. This is as important as providing the 'tools' and apparatus for learning any other subject. Children who feel confident in themselves and their ability are more likely to become independent learners, they are more likely to act independently. The relationship between the child and adults is therefore of central importance in their development. Children need to be given confidence. They should be encouraged to ask questions confidently, and to make their own observations. This is a subject we will return to in Chapter 3; for the time being it will be enough to emphasize that wherever or whenever it is that you find children observing, there is an opportunity for learning. The child may be playing in the sand box; painting a picture; on a visit into town; at the pedestrian lights; using a lift or escalator; discovering some automatic doors; you may be using a bell to stop a bus, whatever it is, if you see that the child is involved they are ready to learn from the experience. Remember the case of Jamie, cited at the beginning of this chapter; when we make the extra effort to understand the child and engage with their talk we will be supporting their learning.

It is also worth remembering that whenever the child makes a choice, a selection, or remarks upon a preference, they have been engaged in some form of 'evaluation'. The terms of that evaluation can therefore be usefully questioned and elaborated. This was vividly illustrated by Dorcas, Iain's daughter, when she was 5:

> Every day on the way to school Dorcas would look at 'the garage'. It was a disused petrol station which had not been modernized. Every day she noted a different aspect of the building . . . the old signs, the tops of the petrol pumps, the fuel lines. Sometimes a detail was noted which triggered a volley of questions, on other occasions she would just look. One morning the demolition crew moved in and Dorcas was distraught. This was a change that she had not wanted and a whole new range of questions emerged. As the new office block was built, each subtle change in the process was noted and commented upon

and a comparison was made in aesthetic terms between the two buildings. She made it clear exactly what she liked and disliked.

We should take advantage of every chance we can to encourage and extend or elaborate these evaluations, but there are also opportunities where children's questions lead us to provide 'explanations'. Apart from concerning ourselves with evaluations and explanations, there are a wide range of things that we can do to support children in developing their *expertise* in designing and making. In the following sections we will explore each of these areas in turn. 'Questioning' will be identified as a key concern.

Developing children's expertise

Learning to evaluate

Children make selections, based on 'evaluations' (applying the proper design and technology terminology), and determine their 'favourites'. They may have a favourite cup and cutlery. This selection may be based on aesthetic or emotional preferences – Does it look good? Does it feel secure/safe? – or its handling characteristics – Does it feel good in my hand? Does it fit the hand or is it easy to lift? They also evaluate food. However in making their choices they are beginning to make judgements based on their own developing criteria. The range of value judgements young children make will also be influenced by adults, siblings and peers. We can usefully invite young children to question these evaluations and to elaborate upon them. They are important because they clearly have meaning for children. They are significant and meaningful to them because they are a part of their reality. All too often we unreasonably invite children to engage with *our* abstractions, but we need to accept their terms, their realities, if we are to support their learning. John Holt (1991: 104) made the point very well:

> Children resist this continual abstracting because their chief business in life is finding and making meaning, putting meaning into a world that must at first seem wholly meaningless to them. It is not a weakness on their part but a strength. They are more passionately interested in reality and meaning than we are, and struggle to preserve it, find it, and invent it, wherever and however they can.

As previously suggested, many everyday experiences, such as shopping, that may be mundane for adults, provide valuable experiences that can be used to enhance children's evaluative capabilities and children's understanding of basic scientific concepts.

Learning to explain

Supporting children's curiosity may provoke questions that are unexpected. We may not be able to answer every question that arises but we can observe with the child and reflect, hypothesize and try out. This will encourage positive attitudes towards science and design technology. Reference books can be used to help us answer some of the questions that arise in our investigating with children (see Appendix 2). We don't have to know everything and we shouldn't be worried that we don't. We must remember that the production of scientific knowledge in the last century has been so great that no one can now be expected to keep up with the subject in its entirety. Increasingly people specialize, and study skills, information handling and information technologies have become more and more important to us all. It is important to recognize that even without a broad knowledge of our own we can promote scientific knowledge and inquiry, and help children develop their scientific skills and attitudes.

Box 1.2 Learning science and design and technology on a shopping trip

Harry returns from a shopping trip with his mum. He helps to unpack the bags hanging from the pushchair handle. Mum explains: 'It is better to do that first, so that Megan [the baby] doesn't tip out. It's all to do with *balance*'.

Tracy helps to carry in the bags and boxes from the car boot. She helps to sort out the shopping and put some things in the fridge and others in the freezer or the food cupboard. In the process of her conversation with Mum she learns that:

- heavier things are carried in the boxes because plastic bags would break;
- perishable foods are kept in the fridge because it's cold;
- food is preserved by freezing, drying and canning.

The notion that designs should be evaluated according to the degree to which they are 'fit for the purpose' is central to design and technology education. The knowledge of food perishability will provide an important precursor to learning about the natural decay of organic materials.

Conversations with parents can lead to children learning all kinds of useful things. Here are some more examples:

- when we put on a cardigan on a cool day (because it keeps in the heat);
- when an old bread crust at the bottom of a bread bin has gone mouldy (because fungi is growing on it);
- when one of the old potatoes in the vegetable rack starts to sprout (because that's how they reproduce themselves);
- when a house plant is wilting (because it hasn't been watered);
- when steam comes from a kettle (because it is boiling).

Learning to design

Designing, as a skill, has been little understood and its importance is therefore often underestimated. As Penfold (1988: 133) has put it, 'designing' calls for a variety of skills: 'motor skills, communication skills, evaluation skills among them. At a fundamental level it has to do with thought and feeling. It involves both linear (logical) and lateral (creative) thinking'.

Much of a child's early development in design happens in the home. Children become increasingly aware, through physical interaction, of the space and the objects that form their environment. Very young children follow patterns of movement utilizing objects within the environment to facilitate their physical development. The toddler through actions, such as using chairs to support their first faltering steps, seems to intuitively assess the best means of using objects within a space. As the child grows their knowledge and use of the space changes.

Box 1.3 Some examples of early design activity

Simon (a 4-year-old) and his mum were watching Rachel (8 months) using the seat of the couch to support herself. She edged her way along the couch to support her walking. Simon suggested moving the chair next to the couch to help Rachel move further along.

I was making an audit of design technology provision in a nursery school. After walking around with a clipboard for an hour or so I looked for a table to rest on while writing. I found a table that was used for technology, one which children could use while standing up. I took a chair and sat at the table. One of the children had been closely observing me and, as I was now stationary, took the opportunity to come and talk. He was most concerned that I was sitting in what appeared to him to be a very awkward position. A discussion developed in which ergonomics and anthropometrics were explored – trying to match chair, table and my body size.

The illustrations show that young children are actually developing an early understanding of ergonomics and anthropometrics. Quality conversations that progressively develop the child's awareness of these two areas can be very successfully achieved in the home. One example might be in selecting the 'best fit';

- in the home or nursery – making a chair 'fit' by piling cushions into a larger chair;
- in the nursery – making a chair for favourite toy figure, doll or teddy.

For many teachers of older children designing is an activity that precedes making an object. Usually this takes the form of a drawing. Often such drawings lack detail. They don't help the child to predict or analyse the problems they may confront in manufacture. Effective design provides the opportunity for predicting and solving aesthetic and functional problems. Young children are actually very good at this but not initially through drawing.

There are two separate issues here that are sometimes confused. On the one hand there is the importance of supporting the child in the design endeavour itself and on the other hand there is a concern for the child to record and communicate their design ideas to others. Increasingly we will want to encourage children to collaborate in their designing and making and eventually we will be anxious for them to evaluate their final products in terms of their early plans. Children's early plans and drawings will provide a standard from which evaluative reviews may subsequently be made. We will want them constantly to ask themselves if the product of their activity fits their original intentions. The development of skills in communicating design ideas through drawing will therefore, ultimately, be important, but these aspects shouldn't cause us too much concern in the early years. At this stage we should support children in developing and testing their ideas through modelling with the materials themselves. In fact young children often find it very difficult to present their design ideas, even in two-dimensional drawings, before they have worked out their solution with the materials themselves. We shouldn't be at all surprised that they need to explore the materials and their properties before making decisions about how the things are going to 'come together'.

Of course there are a number of advantages to using drawings. They can be used by children to help them predict the materials and techniques that they will need; they can also help them to plan and visualize their designs. The point is that there is no reason to assume that this must always be carried out *before* handling the materials. A good deal of this may also be done orally; the child may be encouraged to discuss what they have chosen to construct and they may subsequently be reminded of what they said. We can even draw things *for* children, and this can be especially valuable where we are responding to their own expressed needs, where, for example, they ask for help in designing a working mechanism such as a door or hinge. In these circumstances the child can see how we use the representation to work out a design solution for ourselves and the communicative value of drawing is being demonstrated at the same time. The quality of the learning experience depends crucially upon the child's evaluation of the materials, their planning and their product evaluation. None of these are likely to be given adequate attention unless the educator encourages them in some way. Research shows that even where children are encouraged to draw their designs they are unlikely spontaneously to use their drawings in these ways unless they are made aware of the function of the drawings that they have been instructed to produce.

Learning to make things

Children delight in copying the work of adults and in doing so they are often constructing their own learning. When a child shares in the washing up they may learn about bubbles, floating and sinking, about pushing, upthrust, temperature, the control of temperature. Similarly at other times they can learn a great deal from watching adults using technologies that are less safe for them to handle: a drill, a sewing machine, cooking

---

Box 1.4 Young children learn from everything around them

A prominent early childhood academic tells the story of a 5-year-old girl who became very interested in some work being carried out by the builders that her parents had employed to do some work on a wall in the back garden. She often went out and talked to the builders and her parents could see that they were being very careful about her safety so they encouraged it. The builders even gave her some small bricks of her own and some sand and cement to mix. She was clearly learning a great deal from the experience and her parents were very pleased.

At the end of the week the foreman was handing out the men's pay packets and the child was delighted to find that a packet had been made up for her as well. It contained two five-pence pieces and she was really thrilled. When her father came home from work she could talk of nothing else. He asked her if she was going to finish the job with the builders the following week, but he was distressed to hear her reply: 'Yes we should get it all finished, but only *if* the f***ing bricks arrive'.

controls. They may be watching Mum servicing the car, or Dad making some pancakes and here they are learning about the possibilities open to them when they grow older. We can involve them at these times. Safety is important of course but given young children's acceptance of fantasy, a few quickly improvised props are often enough to allow them to feel entirely involved in helping. Their expectations don't have to be gendered in the ways that ours may have been. This is a subject to which we will return in Chapter 2.

There are many opportunities at home and in nurseries and classrooms to encourage children to practise making things. Sometimes, such as when making a sandwich, we can encourage children to design and make, at other times we may simply provide a design ourselves. They may be building towers with bricks, or tents with some fabric, or animals with Plasticine. Whatever they are making they are learning about materials and structures and different techniques. The most important thing to remember in all of this is to control the level of success. Children need to become more confident, they need to develop their capabilities and not be put off by failure.

Developing children's confidence and interest

Adults often wonder why it is that some children just give up even when they seem initially motivated, while others face similar difficulties and see them as a challenge or as minor obstacles on their way to eventual success. Clearly the answer to this question lies largely in terms of the confidence that a child has developed through his or her experience of confronting similar problems in the past. Their own previous experiences and the skills of their teachers and carers in matching new challenges carefully to their capabilities is highly relevant. Push the child too far and they will fail and lose confidence, get the match right and they will feel achievement and gain in confidence. The most skilled of professional teachers take all of this for granted, it is part of their everyday common-sense educational practice.

We have shown that there are many situations within the home, preschool and the surrounding environments where a child experiences the effects of science and design and technology. Young children often appear to inhabit two worlds, the real and the imagined, and they move quite freely between the two. This is clearly seen when observing young children in imaginative play. Adults can of course be involved in this and it often provides an important opportunity for learning. Barbara Tizard and Martin Hughes (1984) highlighted the role of mothers in encouraging language skills and every adult who has contact with young children can contribute. What makes these interactions valuable in terms of science and design and technology is when the adult encourages the child to ask questions such as, 'Why?' 'What will happen next?' 'Why don't you have a go?' 'I wonder what will happen if . . .?'

We also need to develop children's 'self-questioning' skills. Often when we are playing and working with children we pose a question that can help children to take an idea further or develop a hypothesis, but all too often we miss this chance. Of course there is a danger in using excessive questioning. Brown and Wragg (1993: 18) suggest that there are a number of errors that are common in the way we use questioning with children:

- asking too many questions at once;
- asking a question and answering it yourself;
- asking a difficult question too early;
- asking irrelevant questions;
- asking the same type of question;
- not using probing questions;
- not correcting wrong answers;
- failing to see the implication of answers;
- failing to build on answers.

A great deal has been written about this subject in the context of science education and some of this material will be discussed later. The emphasis here is on talking with children. We need to talk to children about how things are, and about the way that things work. We should talk to them about what they are doing and about what they can go on to do. When talking to children, the trick is to judge the kind of response most appropriate to the situation. There are simple and complex answers to every question and matching the right one to the circumstance and to the child's mood and interest is where the skill lies. This is a subject that we will return to in Chapter 3.

Responding to the differing needs of children

Bronya, finding it extremely boring to have to learn the whole alphabet by herself had taken it into her head to make her sister an experiment in education, to 'play teacher' to her. For several weeks the little girls had amused themselves by arranging, in what was often enough an arbitrary order, their letters cut out of cardboard. Then, one morning, while Bronya was faltering out a very simple reading lesson to her parents, Manya grew impatient, took the opened book from her hands, and read aloud the opening sentence on the page. At first, flattered by the silence that surrounded her, she continued this fascinating game, but suddenly panic seized her. One look at the stupefied faces of M. and Mme Sklodovski, another at Bronya's sulky stare, a few unintelligible stammers, an irrepressible sob – and instead of the infant prodigy there was only a baby of four, crying in a doleful voice through her tears: 'Beg-pardon! Pardon! I didn't do it on purpose. It's not my fault – it's not Bronya's fault! It's only because it was easy!' Manya had suddenly conceived, with despair, that she might perhaps never be forgiven for having learnt to read. After that memorable session the child had grown familiar with her letters; and if she did not make remarkable progress it was owing to the adroit diplomacy of her parents, who constantly avoided giving books to her. Like prudent pedagogues, they were afraid of the precocity of their little girl, and every time she put out her hand toward one of the big-lettered albums that abounded in the house, a voice suggested: 'You'd better play with your blocks'.

(Curie 1942: 9)

Manya Sklodovska was at this time just 4 years of age and she grew up to be known as Marie (or Madam) Curie, the famous scientist. The story provides testimony to the power of play in facilitating learning and one can only wonder about the possible influence of this early encouragement to play with bricks. Young children are highly individual. As Nutbrown (1996) has argued, we may find that one 3-year-old is only able to sort toy animals by colour, while another child may be able to do so by colour and size. This does not mean that we can assume that one child is making more progress than another, however. Children develop at different rates physically, socially, intellectually, emotionally and linguistically and one of the joys of working with infants is that we know that they can make really significant gains in a very short space of time. Every child is an individual, and we should have high expectations for every one of them. But we also need to recognize that just as with other aspects of development, each child's early capability in science and design and technology will vary according to their previous experiences. The task is to identify their existing capabilities and to build upon them.

Children's handicraft skills, their use of tools in particular, are dependent upon a range of fine motor capabilities. Tools such as scissors, files, hacksaws, hand drills, rulers and compasses all need to be gripped, turned, squeezed, pushed and pulled with varying force and hand–eye coordination. The manipulation of components in construction kits demand similar skills. These skills will develop as children are given the experience to practise. This has especially important implications for girls. Boys typically have much greater experience of making models with construction kits. While some efforts are being made to counter adult tendencies to 'gender' toys by organizations such as the National Toy Council, early years educators have a role in actively encouraging girls to play with these tools and materials. It is important to recognize in this respect that to offer equality of opportunity, in terms of equal access and a free choice, will be completely inadequate here. Technology is a National Curriculum foundation subject and all children have an entitlement to be taught the subject in schools. Without attention to the gender differences in preschool experience, however, girls are likely to continue to be disadvantaged. As Brown (1993) has shown, structured provision can be effective in closing the capability gap between boys and girls.

The child's development of fine motor competence, in cutting with scissors for example, is dependent in part upon their development of gross motor facilities in, for example, climbing and balancing. Moreover, as Wolfendale and Bryans (1983) suggest, children who appear 'clumsy' and who are sometimes seen as suffering from 'delayed motor development' benefit considerably from programmes designed to improve their competency. We must be careful to avoid labelling children who lack capability in any specific area. Special needs should be identified at the earliest opportunity and structured programmes developed to support the child.

Box 2.1 Hand–eye coordination

During the preschool years, children develop hand–muscle control in a rather aimless manner, and therefore many children are deficient in the area of fine muscle and hand dexterity . . . The combination of eyes and hands working together is necessary for the achievement of many tasks and experiences . . . Hand–eye co-ordination may be developed through a range of activities from water play and pouring activities, tracing of pathways and shapes, cutting along lines in simple shapes.

(Stewart 1990: 24)

The foregoing arguments suggest that a great deal may be achieved through encouraging exploratory play in working with tools and materials even prior to making things. We will discuss this more fully later in the chapter; first we need to say a little more about how children learn.

'Constructivism': how children learn

When children underperform this is often due to learned helplessness and low self-esteem. This is particularly relevant to pupil self-concepts in key subject areas such as mathematics, science and design and technology. The provision of support and success management, or careful scaffolding, may thus be considered crucial. Smith (1994: 24) identifies three aspects of scaffolding:

1 where the teacher may direct the child's attention to different aspects of a situation;
2 where the child is helped to break down a task into a sequence of smaller tasks which are more manageable;
3 where the teacher helps the child to sequence the steps in the right order.

Cognitive structures or 'schema' as Piaget termed them, are formed as the child first generalizes, as they realize that things are alike – and then discriminates, and as they recognize the essential defining attributes that permit the object to be placed in a particular class or group. Piaget argued that while empirical knowledge might be acquired simply through observation, to learn explanations and concepts we need to self-consciously consider what it is that we do or do not currently *understand* about what we observe. Put simply, from this perspective, whenever we find that an observation is in some way inconsistent with our current understandings, and we are motivated to resolve this inconsistency, we reorganize our schema (our understandings) to accommodate it. This elaborated structure of meaning may then, in turn, be applied to explain the observation and our perception of it is transformed in the process. In a word the learning process is one of 'equilibration'. The process of learning is a mechanism of equilibration, and it is disequilibrium, 'dissonance' or new experience that provides the motor for encouraging the process. The fuel for the motor is provided by the child's 'interest' (DeVries 1997). Learning therefore depends upon new experience and motivation. In young children curiosity is often enough to provide the motivation. This is the essence of 'constructivist learning theory'. We therefore 'make sense' of the world by forming concepts to describe our experiences.

In its most elaborated form, which is probably in the teaching of science (Driver 1983), teaching informed by constructivism is understood to involve a practice where the teacher is first involved in identifying the children's existing understanding and then in providing experiences that develop their understanding further. It is argued that these 'current understandings' are often strongly held, intuitively based, 'common-sense' ideas (Driver 1985). The teacher's task is therefore to provide opportunities for the children to reflect upon alternative (scientific) ideas and experiences that are specifically chosen to challenge their initial understandings. As Harlen (1992) has suggested, it is important to recognize in this that such a challenge must not be so great that the new experiences make no connection with the child's existing frameworks of understanding. In such circumstances they will not progress. Curriculum 'matching' is therefore a very important teaching skill. Any serious mismatch will have severe implications for the child's future self-confidence and motivation in the subject.

If we follow this model we can therefore see that we should always be attempting to encourage a little cognitive dissonance – but not too much. Vygotsky (1962) has provided a complementary theorization that incorporates the notion of a 'zone of proximal development' (ZPD). For Vygotsky this is a zone of capability that extends beyond what the pupil is capable of doing on their own to include those activities they may successfully realize with the support of the teacher or their peers:

> The zone of proximal development defines those functions that have not yet matured but are in the process of maturation, functions that will mature tomorrow but are currently in an embryonic state. These

functions could be termed the 'buds' or 'flowers' of development
rather than the 'fruits' of development.

(Vygotsky 1978: 86)

Yet a number of practical problems have been identified when it comes
to applying the constructivist learning theory in school classrooms and
science laboratories. A major question has been how do we set up situations where a state of dissonance is achieved? Perhaps the biggest problem has been related to the assumptions made regarding the
understandings children bring into the classroom with them. Clearly any
classroom strategy designed to 'correct' a particular 'misconception' is
likely to be of little use to children who have developed others. If we
assumed, for example, that all children of a particular age believed that
only light things floated, we might select a number of heavy pieces of
wood for them to test to challenge their understanding. This wouldn't
help, however, if one or more of the children believed that it was only
wooden things that floated. One way around this would be to set up situations where the children are encouraged to engage with each other's
understandings. It is questionable, to say the least, that we could ever
fully identify the variety of conceptions that are held by a diverse group
of individual children in our preschool settings and infant classrooms. It
is all the more unrealistic to assume that all children of a particular age or
stage of development think the same. It is therefore important for the
teacher to clearly recognize the steps or stages of progression involved in
learning their subject and to apply them, wherever possible, individually.
In Chapter 6 we give concrete advice on how to identify both the stage of
science and design and technology learning the child is currently demonstrating and the next steps to be taken.

There is now widespread acknowledgement of children's early capabilities. Yet developmental stage theory, which was also drawn from Piaget's
work, has sometimes been applied to deny children a range of learning
opportunities until they were considered 'ready'. It is important to recognize in this context that while a distinct series of developmental stages
may be defined, the data that these are based upon relate to the previous
educational experiences of 'typical' children. The 'stages' say little of value
about the potential of children given enhanced educational provision. The
problem is particularly acute for a new subject such as design and technology education, and for the development of investigative science in the
early years where decisions are being made to determine the most appropriate approach to be taken for the first time. We now know that we can
meaningfully discuss problems with young children in ways that make
sense to them (Donaldson 1978; Wood 1988) and we know from our own

experience that young children can achieve a great deal more than they have traditionally been expected to.

Encouraging the interaction of mind and hand

When the child enters the primary school the programmes of study of the National Curriculum for design and technology (DfE 1995a) demand they are taught designing and making skills along with the knowledge and understanding required to realize their designs successfully. Edward De Bono (1977) defined thinking as 'exploring experience for a purpose'. While such explorations may later become more symbolic than concrete, it may well be that some exploration, or play, period, where success and failure are irrelevant, represent an important element in the process of problem solving for young children (Sylva *et al.* 1979). Research conducted with older children suggests that even the simplest 'first hand tactile experiences' invariably involve the child in a process of evaluative reflection. This was effectively described by the Assessment and Performance Unit (1987) as 'an interaction of mind and hand'.

We therefore need to encourage children to try out their ideas with materials, to explore and to prototype, adapt and modify the things they make. Learning theory suggests that games and activities will also be valuable where children note the similarities and differences between materials, where they sort them out and classify them into established groups. Both adult and children's expectations will also be really important. If children produce artefacts that they have made, yet feel little pride in, then it is unlikely that they will be motivated to improve their work further. Failure to do so will lead to discouragement. When children are motivated to achieve quality they will choose to spend longer selecting suitable materials and in developing their ideas before embarking upon the task of making. It will be in these circumstances that early education may contribute towards children's ability to make a positive contribution to a future society. This leads us back to the question of play, the subject with which we began the chapter.

What is play and how can it contribute?

The evidence suggests that play is extremely beneficial in early childhood, particularly in developing social competence. One of the key criteria used by researchers to define 'play' has been that it involves intrinsic motivation (Rubin *et al.* 1983). In practice it is not always easy to distinguish exploration from play, although it has been suggested that specific exploration facilitates convergent (e.g. scientific) learning and that play functions to consolidate that learning and to encourage divergent learning (creativity). In Piaget's terms, exploration provides children with opportunities for active interaction with their environment, and provides an opportunity for them to 'assimilate' new ideas and experiences. Subsequent play provides the possibility of developing their understandings to 'accommodate' any novel ideas or experiences that don't fit in with their current knowledge of the world. For Bruner (1966), play provides an opportunity for the child to 'practise' and gain 'mastery' over new ideas.

A good deal of research has been carried out to study the connection between play and problem solving. According to Pepler (1982) the theoretical models adopted in these studies can be divided into three categories:

1 play as an exploration of the object environment;
2 play as an experience of an experimental and flexible nature; and
3 play as a facilitator of the transition from concrete to abstract thought.

Exploration may be considered a necessary preamble to play, or as an initial stage within play. It may therefore represent an integral part of play or a separate although closely related activity.

In experimenting, the child moves beyond discovering the properties of objects, to determine what they can do with the object. This fits in well with Bruner's (1966) notion of 'mastery'. The importance here of the child being left free from the tensions of instrumental goals is often stressed. This allows for more novel, less inhibited, responses.

For both Piaget (1962) and Vygotsky (1962) play provides the opportunity for children to consider objects abstractly. Children use a variety of props to represent objects. These representations or 'models' of the real world are important in problem solving. The folded paper that signifies for the child an aeroplane soaring through the sky, becomes a 'pivot' for severing the meaning of 'aeroplane' from real aeroplanes. The focus of the child's attention becomes what it is that the object signifies, and can do, its properties and functions, rather than its representation in the real world. The child is therefore able to explore the object in a more abstract and intellectual way. According to Piaget (1962) these early forms of symbolic play provide important precursors for the development of more sophisticated kinds of representational thought later. In these more advanced forms of representational thinking props are no longer required, problems may be solved entirely 'in one's head'.

In terms of educational provision, Tina Bruce's (1991) identification of two distinct ways of thinking about play provides a useful basis for analysis:

1 There are those who see play as educational and as a preparation for future life. They place an emphasis upon adults providing a structure for children's play. The investigation provided in our introductory chapter provides a good example of this. While Brahmajit's jumping provided the initial context, the children's play at 'being scientists' was highly structured (directed) by the teacher.

2 Those who see play as educational yet put an emphasis upon free-flow play and of adults only indirectly providing structure. A good example of this may be where the apparatus (e.g. containers, tools) are regularly changed in a sand tray with the intention of providing a variety of opportunities for the children to 'discover' their properties in their play.

What this account seems to leave out is the ways in which children tend to imitate and direct each other. As Vygotsky (1962) recognized, children structure each others' play all the time. The fundamental difference between many of the approaches to play may in fact simply be concerned with whether or not it should be structured for particular learning ends. An obvious question then arises: does free-flow play on its own constitute simply 'exploration' by the child? If this is the case then it may be justified as an activity in its own right, but 'play' can be seen to provide a separate context for developing learning – a context where particular cognitive 'connections' may be encouraged. As we have seen, and as will be further elaborated, science investigations and design and technology assignments may be considered, and presented as, forms of play in themselves. From this perspective, the scientific or designing and making processes might be considered as the rules for the game. The teacher's role becomes more like that of a coach and a role model, gradually introducing new techniques and challenges that may be employed in the child's problem solving. As Gardner (1991) has argued, educational institutions need to become much more like hands-on museums and schooling (and preschooling), more like serving apprenticeships.

The assumption of 'discovery' has been challenged by a number of writers (Driver 1985; Millar 1989; Siraj-Blatchford 1996), and is now widely rejected: 'Knowledge, in the form of useful generalisations (patterns), does not simply emerge from objective and detailed observation' (Millar and Driver 1987: 50). Sand and water play is often promoted and justified as supporting children's learning in science, but we can easily overestimate what young children learn through these activities. In fact our expectations are often contradictory: While we fail to recognize the quality or significance of the child's observational skills in their day-to-day interaction with the world, we nevertheless expect them to discover phenomena whenever we make the relevant resources available to them.

The teacher, however, needs to provide the (established scientific) scaffolding to help children see and understand what it is they are seeing. Of course this does put a greater emphasis on the educator's own scientific knowledge and in recognition of this fact new entrants to primary school initial teacher education are now required to hold a GCSE grade C or above in science prior to training. For those of us who don't have this kind of background books such as Wensham's (1995) *Understanding Primary Science*, and Farrow's (1996) *The Really Useful Science Book* provide a good deal of valuable background knowledge. The resources listed in Appendix 2 may be even more appropriate in the early years.

In any case, as previously suggested, science is not only about developing children's conceptual understanding, it is also about becoming confident in using methods of enquiry. The key factor in supporting science is the quality of intervention. Even if our knowledge of science is modest we can create a high quality learning environment, one that will enhance children's interest and capability in science and design and technology in the home, in a play group, nursery or infant classroom. As we have seen, a great deal can also be done on an opportunity basis, on shopping trips and outings, in fact anywhere that children engage with their environment. There is no one way to achieve this, and there are many approaches. Our belief is that the most effective methods are those that acknowledge the centrality of the child within this process, that the learning experiences must be appropriate for the individual child or group. Resources may be limited but the trick is to learn as much as you can about them and use them to the full. You will find that a mature hedge or tree within, or adjacent to, your garden or nursery setting will support a host of wildlife. It won't take long to find out about the ecology and even a limited familiarity with the names of plants and 'minibeasts' will impress a young child and show them that there are amazing things to learn about in nature.

Play and creativity

Dansky and Silverman (1973) have shown that play encourages divergent thinking. Anna Craft (1997: 52) has argued that at the core of both science and design and technology:

> is the need for children to think creatively: to experiment, to be open to possibility, to take risks, to be prepared to combine old ways of seeing with new ones, to be prepared to look at a situation or problem in different ways, to seek innovation, to be resourceful.

Craft argues that this requires both right and left-brain thinking and that design and technology in particular requires intuition, spatial orientation, crafts, skills, emotions, expression (all right-hemisphere operations) together with language, sequencing, logic, and mathematical operations (the left-hemisphere operations). She argues that it is important to give children time and space to access the right hemisphere's functions by offering opportunities for them to generate and clarify their ideas through working together, through drama, discussion, modelling, sketching, painting, working with construction kits, and through using information technology drawing and designing packages. While there is still little to be found in the way of convincing research evidence showing that creativity is something that we can formally 'teach', it is clear that we can encourage it (Duffy 1998). The problem may be that for a great deal of the time we do precisely the opposite. We may be doing some work on transport with children, for example, and we may have prepared the glue and taken out the recycled boxes and cardboard wheels for the children to make some models. We ask children to think of something to make but end up discouraging the child

---

Box 2.2 Encouraging creativity

A group of 5-year-olds were encouraged to recount the story of *The Three Little Pigs*. At the end of the story their teacher asked them if they would be as silly as the wolf in climbing down the chimney into the hot cauldron. They were all adamant that they would never have been caught out so easily. The teacher then set the class the task of designing a house that would be too difficult for the wolf to enter 'even if he were as clever as they were'. The children drew their plans as the teacher took out cardboard boxes and other 'found' materials for them to construct their models. The children came up with some amazing designs, some of them clearly inspired by the Road Runner television cartoon series. In all but one case the teacher had predicted the materials required correctly, but one child decided that the best house would be one on the moon! It would have been so easy to discourage the child at this point – instead the teacher called her design to the attention of the whole class and made sure they could see that she was especially pleased with the idea. While all of the other houses, when completed, made up a display on a table in the corner of the classroom, this one house was hung as a mobile above it. Over the next few weeks parents and other visitors would ask about the mobile and the children would explain it to them and share their delight.

Figure 2.1 Gemma's picture

who thinks of the flying carpet because it doesn't fit our plans for the use of the materials. In these circumstances the child is learning that creativity (and divergent thinking) are inappropriate or even 'bad'.

'Identity' and its importance

When we consider the different needs of children we must take into consideration their identity as individuals and a members of various groups. Girls have often been disadvantaged in science, design and technology education in the past, and boys and girls tend to have different scientific and designing and making interests, so the child's membership of a particular gender group is extremely significant. Identity has also been seen as an educational issue when the needs of bilingual and ethnic minority children have been considered. A link has been made between language, culture and identity. The Swann Report (DES 1985: 3), for example, stated that: 'Membership of a particular ethnic group is one of the most important aspects of an individual's identity – in how he or she perceives him or herself and in how he or she is perceived by others'.

More recently, there has been much greater recognition that even chil-

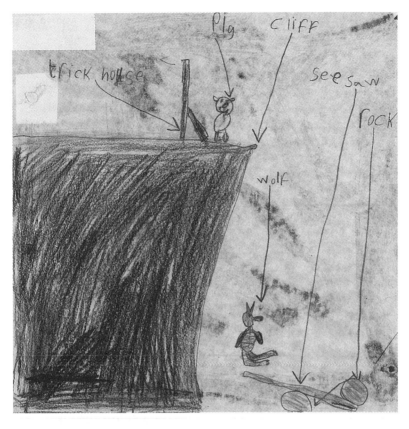

Figure 2.2 Damien's picture

dren of the same gender or ethnic group often have different identities (Hall 1992; Siraj-Blatchford and Clarke in press). Identity is increasingly recognized as a much more complex matter, something conditioned by class, gender and many other experiences that are more or less shared by our membership of other groups in society. Some identity-forming categories such as 'ethnicity' may be socially advantageous or disadvantageous to use in particular circumstances. This explains why different ethnic majority and ethnic minority children, and why, for example, every girl or differently abled child does not see themselves in the same way. Some individuals from disadvantaged groups even hold 'contradictory' positions, so that we should not be at all surprised to find that some girls develop a keen interest in the physical sciences and technology without in any way compromising their femininity. In the same way, individual black and ethnic minority children may be very confident and academically successful in spite of the structural, cultural and interpersonal racism in society.

A number of research studies have identified girls' antipathy to physi-

Table 2.1 Recollection rates for technically-related activities

	Girls (%)	Boys (%)
Making models from kits	6	42
Playing with electric toys	16	45
Creating models with Lego	23	50

Source: Johnson and Murphy 1986

cal science and technology, and there is now a clear consensus among both educationists and industrialists that something needs to be done about this. In technology and the physical sciences girls represent the largest group of underachievers. We know that infants soon form strong opinions about the kind of activities that are suited to boys and girls. As children get older these attitudes become linked to job aspirations and life choices in a very limiting way. A number of studies are now considering the role of boys in this process (See Murphy and Gipps 1996).

We do not need evidence (although plenty is now available) to tell us that boys are encouraged and girls discouraged in science and technology because of their differential leisure activities. The Assessment and Per-formance Unit (APU) asked 11-year-olds about the kind of activities that they had experienced throughout their childhood. As Johnson and Murphy (1986) have argued, the toys, play and games traditionally given to boys clearly provide a more appropriate grounding for later learning in physics (and technology) than girls' toys, play and games.

The APU tests identified problems experienced by the girls in applying physical concepts. This was the only major difference in boys' and girls' attainments. Further tests showed that this discrepancy increases with age. In addition to the influence of toys, play and games we also have the problem of role models. Mothers, older sisters, aunts and grandmothers may not have provided the kind of positive scientific and technological role models that brothers, uncles, fathers and grandfathers have. This can result in a vicious circle reproducing this underachievement, and the negative technological stereotypes are reproduced and even exaggerated in the media. Science and technology can therefore be seen as irrelevant to 'normal' women and girls:

Implicit in much school education and, we might add, gender reform is the notion of 'normal' girls, usually seen to be middle-class and Anglo. Such girls are positioned positively; their culture is made central. They therefore receive an education couched in their own values.

Girls who are not positioned as 'normal' are positioned as other than and less than 'normal' girls. They are seen as different from what is normal and preferable, as special or 'at risk', not because this is how they have been positioned by the schools, but rather because of some sort of dysfunction in their backgrounds.

(Kenway *et al*. 1996: 250)

As Kenway *et al*. (1996) go on to argue this 'sleight of hand' in turn allows the school to shift its responsibility for any problems the girls may have from the school to the home or the culture at large.

Brown's (1993) research with construction sets has already been mentioned; it showed that while there is already a large gap in achievement between boys and girls on entry to formal education, educational programmes can be employed to reduce this gap. In fact Brown showed that there is every reason to believe, that given an effective science and technology education in the early years, girls' underachievement may be eliminated entirely.

As previously noted, children tend to model their behaviour on others who are warm and loving towards them, those who seem to have more power, influence and competence, and those who are seen as similar to themselves. The greatest challenge for educators in the early years may therefore be to provide positive role models in terms of science and design and technology themselves. In practice this would mean showing the children that you have an interest in such things as the classification of plants and animal species, that you investigate when you are curious, and that you enjoy designing and making things for yourself. If we accept the influential nature of this form of learning then it will be even more important to avoid passing on any anxieties that we may have developed ourselves about science and technology.

The problem with 'development'

Science actually has a poor record when it comes to race and gender equality. It was a scientist who argued that women were genetically incapable of thinking scientifically and it was a scientist who first (mis)applied the category of 'race' to human beings (Thorpe *et al*. 1994). We believe that these misconceptions need to be addressed head-on at all stages in education. Appendix 3 therefore provides an outline scheme for tackling the issues in a nursery or reception class. Like many other misconceptions, they have proven to be remarkably pernicious and enduring. As Sandra Harding (1993: 8) suggests:

It has now been forty years since some biologists and physical anthro-pologists began to point out that the concept of race is incompatible with evolutionary theory. They have shown why population genetics should replace the concept of a fixed and discrete cluster of biologi-cal attributes as the empirically and theoretically adequate way to explain human variation. Moreover, it turns out that there is greater genetic variation within every 'racial' group than there is between any two of them. Yet scientists in such fields as biology, medicine, and public health still use this apparently anachronistic concept of race.

In fact the notion of racial inequality is reproduced in, and through, science and design and technology education whenever an implied or explicit assumption of a First through Fourth World continuum of 'development', intellectual sophistication, or 'progress' is taken – that is, whenever we make the assumption that our 'developed' way of life is better than the life led by, for example, the indigenous communities of the Amazon rainforest or Kalahari desert. We can dispute the existence of any such continuum on the grounds of sustainability alone, and yet there is a deeper point to be made here. Science and technology education represent much more than just another valid sphere for anti-racist education. Sci-ence and technology lessons provide more than just one more context in which black children are disadvantaged and global inequalities sustained. Our treatment of science and technology in education and in the wider media has actually provided a major, if not the major support to the most pervasive racist ideologies. Racism occurs when the application of pre-judiced (albeit often unconscious or unintentional) attitudes lead to discriminatory actions. Many, if not most of the white ethnic majority population have grown up to believe themselves to be culturally (if not intellectually) superior to black people. Their 'common sense' (yet totally mistaken) everyday observations appear to confirm their prejudices: they see the relative poverty of Third and Fourth World communities in pre-dominantly technological terms and they infer cultural (and individual) inferiority (Siraj-Blatchford 1996).

In the same way, when it comes to science and technology, boys have grown up to consider themselves superior to girls. Again, their day-to-day observations appear to confirm this. In both cases they deny the 'subordi-nate' groups opportunities, because they imagine that they are inferior. It is the basis of these fundamental scientific and technological prejudices that need to be challenged. If we are to aspire to a more equal society and interdependent and peaceful world we must recognize and celebrate the scientific and technological achievements of Third and Fourth-World cultures and of women. We need to recognize and promote the view that the best solution to a problem is rarely the most complicated and expensive in terms of resources, and that 'feminine' ecological and holistic scientific approaches have significant advantages over more 'masculine' approaches that emphasize reductionism and control.

Research suggests that we should encourage children who have less contact with construction kits, and design and technology activities at home, to participate and play with them in the preschool setting. We should encourage all children to see themselves as aspiring scientists, designers and technologists. We should also be concerned to teach young children about the limitations of 'high' technologies, including their toys, and about the sophistication of home-made toys that have been constructed from recycled materials, and of the toys produced in other cultures. The products of science and technology are all around us and it is never too early to begin educating our children about it. The development of scientific and technological literacy, in this sense, can be seen as an aspect of environmental and citizenship education (Siraj-Blatchford and Siraj-Blatchford 1995). It has a strong moral and ethical component, and as the Schools Council (1975: 4) project on ethics and the environment suggested:

> Effective environmental education cannot rely on appeals to the conscience, to responsibility to fellows and to posterity . . . To become interested in any environmental matter most students need to see how it affects their personal position.

Preschool centres often provide the community focus for a wide range of local campaigns such as those developed to protect children's outdoor play environments, or to provide safe crossing points in high traffic areas. We need to provide good role models and to involve the children. When the children are encouraged to be actively involved in these campaigns they are learning some really important principles of democratic society. They are learning about their place in society, their rights and about their individual responsibilities. Such activities should be extended, in collaboration with parents, as far as possible in the interests of the children's education and of the local community. Examples might include: the provision of disabled access to public buildings; projects concerned with litter and pollution; improvements to public transport; or the promotion of a local ethnic minority arts performance. All of these projects can be tackled, at different levels, with children from 2 or 3 years old onwards.

Developing good practice in early childhood settings

The educational context in which 3-year-old children may find themselves placed for the greater part of a day is subject to great variety. There is currently no coherence in the type of provision for children under 5 years of age in Britain. A parent or carer faced with finding a place for a 3-year-old child may have a number of options available: a workplace nursery, a private nursery, a nursery school, a nursery class within an infant or primary school, a playgroup or social services nursery, or there may be no choice at all. Both the financial circumstances of their family and the region of the country in which they live will have a major bearing on the type of provision that will be available. The approach to educational provision for children under 5 years of age is equally varied and ranges from contexts which are mainly concerned with child care, where there has traditionally been little educational input, to those where education is the primary purpose. Pre-5 providers may base their curriculum for working with young children on a particular philosophical approach such as the Montessori method, High Scope (discussed later in this chapter), some other 'developmentally appropriate' active learning curriculum, or on strategies such as 'free flow' play (see Bruce 1991). The introduction of the *Desirable Outcomes for Children's Learning* (SCAA 1996) is intended to promote a more unified approach to curriculum planning and to assist the development of quality provision for children of 4 years of age. It is probably too early to judge how successful this attempt may be but the place of science and design and technology in these 'desirable outcomes' will be discussed fully in Chapter 5.

The quality of early childhood institutional programmes has been, and continue to be, the subject of a great deal of academic study in the UK and overseas (Sylva *et al*. 1996). Schweinhart *et al*. (1993: 17) provide the following summary of the main characteristics of effective programmes, staffing and administration that have been identified:

- Effective programs use explicitly stated, developmentally appropriate active-learning curricula that support children's self-initiated learning activities.
- Effective teaching staff have been trained in early childhood education and do not change jobs often.
- Effective administrators provide systematic in-service training on site and supervisory support for their staff's curriculum implementation.
- Effective programs maintain classes of fewer than 20 3 to 5-year-olds for every pair of teaching adults.
- In effective programs, staff treat parents as partners and engage in extensive outreach to parents, such as at least monthly home visits, to learn from parents and to help them understand the curriculum and their children's development.

Often early childhood programmes are based on whatever principles were advocated in the training of key staff. The result is a mixture of approaches based on professional training and practical experience. Some aspects of science and design and technology is to be found in the curriculum of many early years educational settings and the introduction of the 'desirable outcomes' (SCAA 1996) has provided an opportunity for this provision to extend to pre-5 provision generally. However given the paucity of guidance in the areas of science and design and technology these are unlikely to substantially change established patterns of working and thus improve the quality of learning in the short term. Hence the need to produce this book.

We consider the approach that we have taken to be one consistent with this series (see Hurst and Joseph 1998), and also with the kind of 'desirable outcomes plus' curriculum recommended by Siraj-Blatchford (1998). As will be clear from the previous chapter, our recommendations for a 'developmentally appropriate curriculum' for science and design and technology are based on assumptions that we hold regarding the individuality of all children. They are based upon the idea that every child comes to us with their own unique set of prior experiences and their own distinct identity.

Yet one of the most significant realities of professional development is, as Fleer and Hardy (1996) have noted, the fact that any attempt to graft a radically different approach will be met by significant problems associated with understanding and implementation. Practice development needs to be built upon individual strengths and upon existing areas of confidence. In common with Fleer and Hardy, we therefore promote a developmentally appropriate, individualized and interactive approach, but continue to recognize the contribution of other educational approaches. There is a good deal to be learnt in teaching science and design and technology and for those of us who are professional educators the process of learning will engage us throughout our careers. As Fleer and Hardy say, one of the most important ways that we can pursue our own professional development is by working with other educators. At the end of the day, however, it is important to recognize that it will all depend upon our personal commitment:

> The continuing development of your competence and confidence in the teaching of science [and in design and technology] education will be based on the level of your commitment to the view that science [and design and technology] education can, and should be, an essential component of the education of all children. At its best, science [and design and technology] education can enrich and empower people in key aspects of their life. Science [and design and technology] can help in the development of our understanding of our existence as humans in our complex and wonderful universe.
>
> (Fleer and Hardy 1996: 194)

We need to be clear in our minds what the benefits are and be ready to promote science and design and technology with our colleagues. Appendix 2 includes a number of resources; Bronowski's (1979) *The Ascent of Man* and Pacey's (1994) *The Culture of Technology* are especially powerful. Bunch and Hellemans' (1993) *The Timetables of Technology* and Asimov's (1987) *New Guide to Science* are also likely to be influential.

Developmentally appropriate curriculum (DAC)

While we explicitly offer a developmentally appropriate (see Chapters 1 and 2) approach to the curriculum we are fully aware that this whole notion of DAC has been brought into question (see MacNaughton 1995). In fact we believe the critique may have been justified to the extent that it has sometimes been suggested that a particular set of classroom or nursery practices could be defined as objectively appropriate for all children at a certain stage of their development. Although by no means an unproblematic idea in itself, the major problem has not in fact been with the understanding of 'development' that has been employed but rather that of 'curriculum'. Curriculum is often understood as a syllabus or as a set of educational proposals and plans, but educational theorists have taken the idea of curriculum much further in recent years to conceptualize it in a range of different ways. Stenhouse's (1978) perspective has been especially influential, where curriculum is seen as an evolving product, something that should always be seen as specific to a particular time and place and as an hypothesis testable in practice by teachers or other educators working as 'reflective practitioners'.

If we adopt this view, and we think that we should, then we recognize the importance of teachers and carers taking on the responsibility for developing an appropriate curriculum on a day-to-day basis as a central part of their educational role. We accept that every child is different and argue that it is crucial that we recognize the need to respect each child as a unique individual. The alternative is to assume that we can somehow define some general characteristics of children's thinking at a particular age. Yet this is impractical, we are entirely unable to predict the prior lived experiences of all of the children in our care. While developmental psychology has told us a great deal about how children learn, it can offer no clear guidance on what or how to teach. We cannot know in advance exactly what knowledge and understanding the children bring with them into the classroom or preschool setting and we must therefore develop practical approaches to supporting them that build on a wide variety of children's experiences in a meaningful way.

Factors that determine quality

'Quality' in the specific context of science and design and technology in the early years is difficult to describe. As with quality provision for young children generally we can usually recognize it when we see it. In some ways it is easier to start by describing what is not so good in general practice and to draw conclusions from this about quality provision. One of our students provided us with the following account of the experiences of a 5-year-old:

> On my first teaching practice, in a vertically grouped infant class, the children were allowed choices of activity in the afternoon. This was to allow the teacher to concentrate on hearing readers or whatever. There was always a 'junk modeling table' out with the same things on it each day – boxes, more boxes, scissors, glue, cardboard etc. Every day Darren came to this table and every day he made the same thing. At the end of the session the model would go in the bin. Towards the

end of the second week I went to Darren and asked what he was making. He said he wanted to make a truck but couldn't make one because the wheels wouldn't move. I realized that he would not move further on in the process until he had been helped to find a way to solve his problem.

Until Darren was provided with a solution (e.g. a simple wheel and axle system made up from cotton reels held on to dowelling with tap washers), he could make no progress at all in his designing and making.

A teacher on one of our training courses also made an important observation when he commented that, 'You can always tell good early years technology because the pile of cardboard on the table doesn't look very different from the pile on the floor'. The comment may have been made flippantly but this suggestion does warrant consideration. First, if a purpose of design technology in the early years is for children to experiment with materials and tools then surely they should not always be constrained by an overemphasis on the finished product. The tangle of card, paper and glue on the table may not look like very much to the adult but it may have meaning to the child, and they may have learnt a few things in making it. This may appear at odds with the common practice found in many early years settings where numerous identical products are made for the children to take home. In these cases the creativity and skill of the children is often restricted to picking up one prepared component (e.g. a ready-painted egg-container daffodil) and gluing it onto another (e.g. a ready-made card). The tangle may provide the context for greater learning but the high quality product may develop confidence and encourage motivation. Educators have often felt faced with a decision between the two and yet, as is often the case with 'apparent' dilemmas in education, the answer is for us to encourage both: we should take a balanced approach that allows the children to build up their confidence in producing high quality finished products and at the same time provide time for experimenting and playing freely with materials. It is worth remembering that even the assembly of ready-made components that have been produced by an adult constitutes a legitimate form of design and technology when the child is invited to adapt the product in some way to their own purposes.

A key area of quality relates to knowledge and understanding. Children need to know how to achieve the effect wanted, to understand what materials and tools to use and to have a degree of control over the process. Adult support and intervention is crucial but need not dominate the activity. When motivated, young children often prove to be extremely resourceful. This can be illustrated by 5-year-old Josh's experience of making a caterpillar:

Josh liked the *Hungry Caterpillar* story [by Eric Carle]. He joined lots of tubes but ran out of the short treasury tags he was using to fix them (see Chapter 6). He found a few long ones but didn't like the way they joined the tubes together. He tried pushing one end of the treasury tag through the hole at the other end of the tube, but the treasury tag was not long enough to fit. He then tried using masking tape to hold it in place. The piece was too small and pulled off when the caterpillar was pulled along. A longer piece was used. Finally it worked.

The quantity and quality of resources that we provide are important but they do not in themselves ensure a good experience for children. A very limited range of resources can be effective if used with careful planning. An example of making umbrellas in an inner city nursery may help to illustrate this. The example also provides an illustration of curriculum integration, and this is a topic we will return to later. The majority of children who chose to join the activity were 4-year-olds although there were some rising 4s within the group. The nursery was following a topic related to science at the time: the weather and seasons. The teacher was also keen to focus the project on the development of the children's personal and social education, their self-esteem and the children's consideration of the needs of others as well as on their design and technology.

In preparation for the activity, both the parents and children were encouraged to look at umbrellas at home and where possible to bring one into nursery. All of the resulting conversations, explorations, evaluations and investigations developed the children's understanding and knowledge of umbrellas. They learnt about:

- their purpose as a protector – from both the sun and the rain;
- how they are used;
- about their size and shape;
- about selecting umbrellas and personal choice;
- and about umbrellas as an indication of rank and status (important people).

This final aspect was supported by photos of Ethiopian priests with umbrellas (several Rastafarian children attended the nursery), also paintings of Indian Mughal princes in howdahs with umbrellas on elephants.

The first focused practical activity took place on a Friday afternoon. It began with an evaluation of a golfing umbrella. All of the children who elected to join the activity were invited to come under the umbrella and to note how many children could get under without hurting each other. This involved the children in negotiating space, being aware of others and cooperating. The organization that was required to get the children out from under the umbrella proved just as difficult!

Then, with the children sitting around the umbrella, the children inspected and commented on the structure and evaluated the opening mechanism:

- how did it open and close?
- how could we control it?
- what made it stay up?

The children were then invited to look at other umbrellas and many did, at home over the weekend. The next week the evaluation was followed up when the children were given the opportunity to make their own umbrellas. They had access to a restricted range of tools; to single-hole punches, scissors and snips. The materials were those commonly found in any nursery; paper, tissue, card, fabric, cellophane and aluminium foil. Cardboard tubes, artstraws, pipe cleaners and florist's wire were also available. The fixings and fasteners available were limited to Sellotape, masking tape and PVA glue. It was mostly the 4-year-olds who decided to make umbrellas, and when the children had finished the umbrellas all worked. The most important element was recognized as being the lifting mechanism;

Figure 3.1 Well at least I'm going to stay dry

Figure 3.2 Cherise's sunshine umbrella

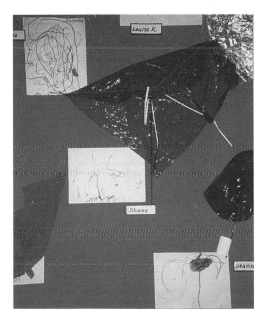

Figure 3.3 Umbrella designs

the children's solutions in making a working mechanism turned out to be very different. The children's justifications for their choice of materials showed some interesting patterns of thought. Cellophane and foil were more popular than paper and fabric, even though these materials were more difficult to manipulate. The general feeling was that they were good because they were shiny – and waterproof.

The mechanism, the movable 'ring' that moved the spokes attached to the umbrella covering, was produced in a number of ways. The adults supported the children by helping them focus their observations in thinking about these mechanisms. Several children used card tubes. In one case the tube was cut lengthways and squashed to make it narrower. Other solutions included paper squashed to form a tube, and a pipe cleaner ring taped onto the florist wire spokes. Some of the umbrellas were taken home the following weekend and reappeared on Monday with modifications and additions. The children were also encouraged to make explanatory design drawings to go alongside their displayed work.

The products of the activity provide an indication of quality, but the support that was offered by the staff at each stage of the work provided an even more significant indication. Also:

- The work was relevant and set at a level indicating the staff had high expectations of the children.
- Science, design and technology were combined very effectively within an even broader integrated curriculum.
- The introduction was paced over a period of time, allowing the children to become familiar with the artefacts and their use.
- A focus was constantly placed on specific features of the golf umbrella; these focused conversations allowed an understanding of the mechanisms and structure to develop at an appropriate pace.
- Support was provided for the children to explore, learn and play at their own pace.
- Every child's work was different. They used different materials and could give reasons for their choice (including some that were entirely unexpected).
- Every child responded at some point in the process to offer a contribution.
- The children used their knowledge of the mechanisms and structures effectively. They also demonstrated their understanding of why things happened.
- Previous work in design technology, the use of snips and hole punches

on a variety of materials, was fully exploited and the children made appropriate use of equipment.

• The children were engaged in designerly play, they were being 'designers and technologists', trying out and rejecting many ideas as they went along.

An interesting feature that was common to all of the umbrellas was that they moved. The stays of the umbrellas were made differently and from different materials, there was variety in the way that they were connected to the central stick and to the covering and yet they all moved. Similar work undertaken elsewhere without any of the preparatory and continued focus on the structure and mechanism of the umbrella resulted in umbrellas that were similar in form but produced no movement.

Developing practical approaches to support learning in science

An important factor in the success of any approach to supporting learning in the early years is the enthusiasm and commitment of the individual or team. Differences of approach will affect children's experience of science and design technology and the experience offered to children may also be limited by a range of other factors, including the facilities available, the adult's interest in and knowledge of the subjects, and their empathy for, and philosophical commitment to, teaching young children. The apparent ease with which some infant teachers have taken to science in the past may be because the investigative processes match methods of inquiry that are well established in early years education.

Feasey (1993) has suggested that scientific processes of inquiry should develop through five steps. These are consistent with the constructivist approach discussed in the last chapter:

1 examining the similarities (e.g. between objects that sink – float, those that stick together – those that don't);
2 choosing appropriate equipment for that observation (e.g. lenses, balances etc.);
3 focusing on key points (weight, shape, size, colour, slipperiness);
4 using a range of senses in doing so;
5 using scientific knowledge to make use of the observations (e.g. concluding that shiny things stick together and testing it, suggesting that things that stick together are metal and testing that).

Defining the processes in such a structured way may appear to preclude children from learning science 'without realizing it'. We don't believe that.

We believe that it is important for children to realize that they are learning science, but it is even more important that teachers understand the aspects of science that they are teaching. As was suggested in Chapter 2, this means that the teacher cannot simply present or expose children to situations that may or may not trigger scientific thinking and expect them to discover or understand the underlying concepts.

Opportunities and constraints in design and technology

In identifying the opportunities and constraints in design and technology we can usefully begin with another concrete example of practice. How typical is this case study of your experience?

The play group staff encouraged children to select their own programme of activities. In this context children's work in design and technology was presented as 'partially supervised (recycled) box modelling'. In other curriculum areas there was direct instruction, but in this activity there was none. At specific times of the year supervised activities were undertaken; for Mother's Day, for Christmas and other festivals cards were made according to a 'recipe'. For the box modelling, intervention was generally limited to either safety issues – with the scissors, for example – or for economy – restricting the amount of glue used.

The children were given free access to a limited range of recyclable materials that were mainly boxes and tubes. There was no system to the storage of resources and this restricted the range of materials. These resources were placed on a table for them. A comprehensive range of collage materials were available however. The use of tools was unduly restricted as the staff lacked confidence and were concerned about safety. Planning for the activity was minimal. Children were simply encouraged to make things using their imagination as a stimulus using recycled materials or construction kits. Parents often acted as helpers – working unsupervised with their own children and with others.

A common objective of the staff was to encourage children's independence, but the way in which this was thought to be achieved differed between staff. One member of staff thought that the best way to encourage independence was through example – 'showing children how to do things'. Another member of staff thought children should 'just enjoy themselves – they will get enough of being taught later on.'

Two of the children observed in this context did exhibit a high degree of independence. Nathan spent a long time at every session playing with the materials. The forms that his work took varied from day to day; often he would spend a lot of time trying to join things together with glue, but without success. When Sellotape was available far less frustration was evident. Definite themes seemed to develop related to his family members and their dog. He was quite keen to talk during the making process and this usually related to what was being made. Kylie also made full use of the materials but always seemed to have an object in mind before she embarked on making. This rarely developed into anything recognizable to anyone else, but it seemed to satisfy her. Handling the glue, she explored the swirls and lumps that she could make and this engrossed her for some time before she began the joining of boxes.

The quality of experiences for these children could be enriched at times with little expenditure, with a change in focus on learning objectives. The children would have benefited from a better planned and coordinated curriculum. They would have made better choices in their selection of materials if the options were clearly identified for them. They would also have benefited from direct instruction in the use of tools and from some direction, or collaborative definition of their designing and making projects.

Children respond to, use, and manipulate technology from an early age but there is often a lack of continuity between what many children experience at home and the experience they have in their playgroup, nursery or infant classroom. This sometimes creates major barriers to the development of their capability in science and design and technology. Young children love to make things and they are often highly motivated by 'making' activities. Even when children have sophisticated toys at home they tend to make use of any object that comes to hand in their imaginative play. The motivation may spring from a wish to make something for a particular purpose, in technological terms, to create a specific product. This may be a prop for their imaginative play or something for another purpose, such as a card or a gift. This identification of the need to make something, and of thinking what the product will be and how it will be used, is an important aspect of the child's initial understanding of the technological process.

Play and design are inextricably linked. As suggested in Chapter 2, children's use of props in symbolic play is significant in their development. Because of the symbolic nature of many of the children's designed products, an object that has been made to fit a specific purpose can later be discarded if it does not meet the required need. Props have always been an important part of play and many adults can remember vividly their experiences of making tents from a sheet draped over a clothes horse or using a box as a doll's bed:

> When I was about 6 years old and my sister 4, we used to enjoy play-ing games where we imagined we were grown ups and could do whatever we wanted to do. These games quite often took place after we had been shopping with our parents for the simple reason that this was when we got the equipment we needed. We would use the big cardboard boxes that my parents transported our weekly groceries in to build cars or space ships. We used to sit in the boxes and imagine we were astronauts flying throughout space. Occasionally my older brother would join in by pulling and pushing our boxes along the corridor, with us still sitting inside them. We would imagine that the flaps on the boxes were wings.
>
> (Tamsin, age 18)

Adult intervention in this type of play must be sensitively handled, the wrong comment at the wrong time can stop the flow. At appropriate times, perhaps outside of the immediate play context, the introduction of new materials may provide ideas for children to adapt their play when they feel that it is appropriate.

Curriculum planning for individual needs

Nursery classes, particularly those attached to infant or primary schools, have felt the impact of the National Curriculum for some time and this has influenced the way in which the curriculum is interpreted. In some nurs-eries the curriculum has become a means of delivering a curriculum that is seen as a preparation for Key Stage 1. This is more frequently seen in schools where whole school policies for curriculum areas have been developed at an early stage. At times an inappropriately diluted version of National Cur-riculum Key Stage 1 science and design and technology is applied. But for a curriculum to be developmentally appropriate for the individual child, the key experiences of home life, which is, in effect, the majority of their life experiences so far, should be acknowledged and fully utilized.

The sort of curriculum that we are advocating is therefore a balanced one that draws on a range of different emphases and approaches, that is developed collaboratively with the individual child's needs in mind. The notion of curriculum breadth is important, as in our opinion there are few areas of learning that should be excluded entirely. While we would therefore agree with most practitioners that an early emphasis on formal literacy and numeracy may be detrimental, we also feel that there are valu-able opportunities to develop children's pre- and emergent literacy and numeracy knowledge through science and design technology (see Feasey and Siraj-Blatchford 1998). Practical, process based activities can provide a valuable platform for early language and number development even (or rather especially) where the language of the home is not English.

The initial introduction of a four-attainment National Curriculum for design and technology encouraged a process model to be adopted in designing and making (Siraj-Blatchford and Coates 1995). This is adapted in Chapter 4 to provide an appropriate process model for the early years. The use of this kind of model is particularly apt given its congruence with the High Scope 'plan–do–review' methods with which some early years practitioners may be familiar. In the following pages the approach will be outlined in some detail, although we would like to re-emphasize at this point our intention is *not* to prescribe any one magic method, but rather to encourage practitioners to make a selection of those aspects most appropriate (at the time) for use with their particular children and early childhood setting.

High Scope

For those less familiar with the methodology, the High Scope project is based upon what Weikart *et al.* (1971) termed *The Cognitively Orientated Curriculum* in the USA in the early 1970s. The essential features of the High Scope daily routine are best presented in the words of Hohmann *et al.* (1979: 59–60):

Planning time – Children decide for themselves what they're going to do during work time. They indicate their plans to the adults, who help them think through and elaborate their ideas and also record their plans for them and help them get started.

Work time – Children carry out the projects and activities they've planned. Adults move among them, assisting and supporting them, extending their ideas. Children who complete their initial plan make and work on another.

Recall time – Recall time is the third element of the plan–do–review cycle. Small groups of five to eight children meet together with an adult to recall and represent their work time activities; often this is done while the children are having their snack.

Another four key times are defined with the suggestion that each is arranged into a daily routine that suits the relevant timing and scheduling constraints.

Clean-up time – Children store their unfinished projects and sort, order and put away materials they've used during work time.

Small-group time – During small-group time the children work with materials, usually chosen by the adult, in an activity designed to allow the adult to observe and assess children in terms of a particular key experience. A small-group activity might, for example, involve each child making his [sic] own batch of playdough and observing changes that occur, or each child building with boxes and blocks to explore the different ways objects can be arranged.

Outside time – Children and adults are involved in vigorous physical activity – running, throwing, swinging, climbing, rolling. As in all activities, adults encourage the children to talk about what they are doing.

Circle time – All the children and adults meet together as a large group to sing and make up action songs, play musical instruments, move to music, play games and sometimes discuss an upcoming special event.

(Hohmann *et al*. 1979: 59–60)

Many of the features of this approach have been adopted in this book, many have also been adapted and many extended to support the specific curriculum focus. As previously suggested, our intention has not been to encourage anyone to graft a radically different approach; we have made

---

Box 3.1 Plan–do–review

A key worker, the teacher or nursery nurse, meets with their group of children. They encourage the children to discuss and to jointly plan a 'making' task. The adult provides the framework from which the children can develop their own approach to the learning task. This initial planning activity allows all the participants to explore the issues, to ascertain their needs and understand the purpose of the task. This activity also allows the key worker an opportunity to gauge the level of support that would be appropriate for each individual child's learning and level of understanding/capability.

The 'doing' activity takes place in an area that has been specifically designed to support children's independent learning. Resources are readily obtainable from shelves at child height, clearly marked so that they may be replaced when they are no longer required. The children work through the activity at their own pace with appropriate support and guidance.

Finally the work is reviewed, the adult draws the group into discussion of their learning; this constitutes an evaluation, a sharing. The role of the key worker will be to emphasize the qualities inherent in each of the products, the connections in the learning context, to develop self-confidence in the children, and to prepare them for the next steps.

our selection from the ideas available and we hope that our readers will make *their* own selections.

Planning and effective questioning

Planning may involve making lists, drawing ideas, talking about intentions. If we are to support the children in their work we need to find out what their intentions are and what skills, knowledge and understandings they can draw upon in pursuing them. If we are to help children to develop their own planning skills we also need to ask them how they will begin, what they intend to do next, and about how they will know when they are finished. We should help them recognize this as a significant stage in the science and design and technology process and that problems can often be overcome if they are foreseen.

Adults at home and in nursery often plan work with young children. In preparing and cooking food (food design and technology) adults often lead children through the preparation process. On such occasions questions are often structured to involve children as active participants in the planning. What we want is for the children to develop their own questions, and as Craft (1997) argues, one way to get them started is to first ask them questions. The questions need to be closely related to what the children are already thinking. They need to develop confidence in their own ideas; the use of 'open' questions in particular can help in this. Craft (1997: 47) clarifies the point:

> 'Open' questions have lots of possible answers, not just one correct one. They often begin with 'Why' or 'What' or 'How' . . . Open questions allow children to voice their own ideas. They also allow you to hear what the children have noticed, and what they consider important. Open questions also encourage children to get involved in the process of investigation. On the other hand, 'closed' questions are ones where there is one correct answer. These questions often have a 'Yes' or 'No' answer, or a specific place, description, name or time. They often begin with words like 'Where' or 'When' or 'Is it'. For example, 'Where is your knee?' or 'When does chocolate melt?' or 'Is the light bulb on?' In scientific investigation and experimentation, you need to use both open and closed questions. Closed questions can help children to observe what is happening. Open questions can help them to work out why that is.

As Craft says, it is inevitable that children will often come up with questions that are impossible to investigate in the classroom. There are also many questions that children will ask that nobody has yet found a way to answer. It is therefore often necessary to be intellectually honest, and to tell children that we don't know. This doesn't need to be negative – it can easily be accompanied by speculation about how someone (perhaps the child) will someday find a way to answer it. At the same time we need to recognize a question with potential, one that provides a good opportunity to follow through in the classroom. Another strategy is to create opportunities for children to ask questions as a structured element in science and design and technology work. Having generated the questions, you encourage the children to decide which ones are testable, and then how they might test them.

Even large groups of children can be actively involved in this planning stage when you are embarking on whole class projects. The adult facilitator can take notes of an initial brainstorming session of children's ideas, thereby providing a written record. They can also support the planning by suggesting, directing and drawing out the children's ideas and perhaps producing them as a poster that may provide a starting point for a project such as designing a new play area (see Box 3.2).

Encouraging children to design things to satisfy the needs of others is sometimes difficult. Roleplay provides one solution to this problem. It actually represents an important part of a child's early learning. In roleplay the child can pretend to be another person, an animal or even an object. They enter into a world that is entirely within their imaginative control. In some ways this kind of play, although initially egocentric, provides an introduction to the needs of others. In roleplay children share common experiences; they bring individual insights of the designed world, a world influenced by scientific applications and technological aids.

As children extend their roleplay into more social and interactive involvement, the adult can extend the child's range and depth of experience. A roleplay area in the nursery or classroom provides a context in which all adults can support the development of science and design technology through 'real' experience. If children are involved in the planning and setting stage they become more active users. Ownership of the area also means that children feel that they can make changes to meet their needs. Moving from a situation where there is a static roleplay area to one in which regular change occurs does demand extra planning but the advantages for children's learning are far reaching.

Imagining being another someone or something else in roleplay can be a means of considering the needs of others. It helps to develop an ability to recognize that different people have different needs (e.g. medical, nutritional, emotional). For example in a nursery where only one child wore glasses, there were problems of verbal bullying. This was addressed by the staff making glasses with children.

Designing and making play environments

In planning an environment, a new shop for the roleplay area, or a redesigned home corner, the children will be making decisions. They will decide on the essential components of the environment and where they should be placed. Within the environment they may design and operate systems. They may use toy or educational supply equipment or they may design and make their own resources.

An important outcome of this activity would be a heightened awareness of space and its use. Children have to cooperate to be able to use the limited space effectively; they will learn the need to negotiate and to arrange their resources so they can be used fairly and efficiently. In other words they will be learning how to operate technological systems. As children become familiar with the routine of setting up an environment for play they will begin to learn skills of negotiation.

'Doing' science and design and technology

The provision of a wide range of readily accessible resources encourages children to assess and select materials for making. The misuse of the word

---

Box 3.2 Designing a new play area

The home corner in the nursery was a mess, children dashed in and out and no 'quality' play was taking place. What were the reasons for this lack of interest? Could it be that the children felt no involvement, no ownership for the area – or was it just boring?

A new area was set up in another part of the nursery. A story about an octopus was used as a starting point. An octopus was made from newspaper, card tubes, treasury tags and paper fasteners and suspended from the ceiling. This was a large project for the children who found it difficult to work together as a group. Design technology had been an activity undertaken by individuals rather than as a collaborative activity in the past. During the weeks that followed the children identified and provided for the needs of the octopus. A house was erected around it, large sheets of card were laced together and suspended from the ceiling, a door and a (hinged) window were made so that 'it could see out' and people could come and visit. The legs became sound makers, different sounds for each leg, so that it could 'talk'. Morning and afternoon groups made modifications which were investigated by each other. The house became a place to drink milk, tell stories, read books and for parents and children to play.

'model' has created many problems for teachers. The word is often used when referring to a finished product, something made by a child. In design and technology, however, a 'model' is a prototype, a preparatory stage of making. Modelling for a child should mean 'sorting out ideas', playing with materials in a deliberate way to investigate the qualities of materials, to explore ideas when making things. We can model imaginatively by drawing, by joining things in different ways, by trying different sizes and shapes for sandwiches; in fact all the preliminary experiments carried out during the making process constitute models. We can't see children's ideas – not until they begin to model, then the imaginative source is translated into visible clues. A few well chosen questions at this stage will give us some insight.

While children make things they constantly evaluate; they choose one method and not another; they select one material rather than another; they use a range of criteria that may sometimes appear bizarre to an adult. The child may select something that glitters, is not too small and difficult to pick up. We may not always be able to identify their criteria but they are criteria none the less. One of our most significant aims must be to encourage them to adopt ever more sophisticated criteria.

Reviewing and evaluating: working in partnership

Evaluation takes place within most process based activities; in science it forms an essential part of investigation; in design technology it is carried out during the process and when a product is completed as a 'product review'. This kind of end product review often provides a very useful starting point for a design and technology project, where the child evaluates a number of possible outcomes or solutions to a problem before beginning to model their own. Children begin to make informed evaluations with the help of adults who guide, point out and act as a sounding board for ideas. This role is more effective when adults working as a team, in a nursery or playgroup, use a common approach. This is also true of collaboration between parents and practitioners.

Sharing children's evaluative responses with other adults within the educational context helps to provide a wider based scaffolding for children. It ensures that these shared experiences can be communicated to parents who may observe similar patterns of questioning at home. This may evolve into an effective two-way communication and aid the development of adults' as well as children's critical questioning skills. Parents and other carers often play a role in early education that is not fully developed: the recognition and encouragement of areas of children's interest.

Box 3.3 Making a car engine

Much of the design and technology work at this nursery had tended to be small scale. The storage of materials was considered a problem and the children had little free access. For that reason the children rarely experienced making large three-dimensional pieces. Yet given free access to masking tape, an unexpected supply of double-sided tape, and some large boxes and tubes, this 4-year-old extended her play into making her own props. As her favourite activity at home was helping her dad with the car, she used this experience in her modelling. To the uninformed onlooker this picture may appear to show a collection of boxes and a large tube. It is in fact a car engine, complete with wiring . The tube is a gear stick with a knob on the end (the yogurt pot), which rotates in the box base. The child decided against cutting the tube down to a more manageable size as she enjoyed moving it with two hands.

Figure 3.4 A model car engine

At this early age children's modelling is not as strongly influenced by their gender as it usually later becomes. The memory of a positive experience in making something like an engine may therefore be influential, leading her to reject the stereotypes in later years.

An integrated approach to science, design and technology education

As previously suggested, in the early years of education it is essential that we aim to relate learning to the child's own experience and this in turn must relate both to the child's previous knowledge and understanding, their developing physical capability and moral awareness. We have argued that in teaching it is always important for the teacher to clearly recognize the steps or stages of development (progression) involved. In National Curriculum school science this involves the concepts concerned with 'life processes and living things', 'materials and their properties' and 'physical processes' (see Appendix 4). With design and technology in schools it most significantly includes progression in the schemas (concepts) relating to structures, mechanisms and products and applications, yet the very same principles apply in the development of investigative and problem-solving schemes and in the young child's early learning about the nature of science and design and technology. The SCAA (1996: 50) *Desirable Outcomes* for children entering compulsory education at 5 suggest that children should be able to:

1 Explore and recognize features of living things, objects and events in the natural and made world;
2 Look closely at similarities, differences, patterns and change;
3 Talk about their observations, sometimes recording them and ask questions to gain information about why things happen and how things work;
4 Explore and select materials and equipment and use skills such as cutting, joining, folding and building for a variety of purposes;

5 Use information technology, where appropriate, to support their learning.

As we have seen, exploration should help develop the child's observation skills and these in turn should support the development of skills in sorting, sequencing and recognizing relationships. All of these skills are employed in experimental and investigative science. Following their entry into school at the age of 5, the National Curriculum, at level one, expects pupils to be able to: 'describe simple features of objects, living things and events they observe, communicating their findings in simple ways, such as by talking about their work or through drawings or simple charts' (DfE 1995b: 50).

The National Curriculum expects children, by the age of 7, to be able to respond to suggestions, put forward their own ideas and sometimes make simple predictions. They are also expected to make relevant observations and measure quantities, such as length and mass, using a range of simple equipment. With some help they should be able to carry out a fair test, recognizing and explaining why it is fair. They should record their observations in a variety of ways and provide explanations for observations and where they occur, for simple patterns in recorded measurements. They should say what they have found out from their work. This might be considered a steep learning curve but where the kind of 'desirable outcomes plus' (Siraj-Blatchford 1998) curriculum that we outline here is followed, a good deal of valuable preparation can begin in the preschool.

No specific guidance is given in the *Desirable Outcomes* (SCAA 1996) regarding the scientific knowledge that might be considered appropriate to introduce to children in the preschool, and at what stage this is appropriate. What we should be aiming to do at this stage is to give children a first understanding of what scientific knowledge *is.* This is best achieved by introducing established scientific knowledge when the children ask the appropriate questions. As we suggested in Chapter 1, appropriate questions may be encouraged and careful preparation and/or good reference material provides a means of satisfying the child's curiosity and demonstrating the authority and value of established scientific knowledge.

In the school, children will also need to be progressively introduced to more complex problem-solving and investigative strategies so that they can draw upon these independently in their future work. A simple example may be taken from mathematics, where we first teach children algorithms (set procedures) to solve simple problems of multiplication and long division. At the early stages of writing, we also suggest to pupils that they structure a story by first setting a scene, then identifying characters, describing some action, and finally composing an ending. The use of phonics provides another example: we teach pupils to sound out words and connect particular sounds to particular graphic symbols. All of these represent different forms of 'heuristic model' and the value of heuristic models in education has long been recognized. Some explanation of the term may be useful. In the following pages we will offer our own heuristic models to educators in supporting children's investigation and their designing and making.

Heuréka!

The word heuréka has been corrupted to 'eureka' in English; it was the Greek word for 'I have found'. This was the same word that Archimedes is said to have exclaimed on leaping from his bath. When Archimedes was asked to advise the suspicious king (Hiero II of Syracuse) on the true composition of his allegedly solid gold crown he was, at first, unsure how to tackle the problem. The problem was that Archimedes did not know how to measure the volume of such a complex irregular artefact. Then he applied a 'concept' that provided a solution. According to the story, he was taking a bath and he noticed that the water rose as he climbed in. It was only then that he realized how it was that he could measure the volume, and calculate the specific gravity of the crown. He would immerse the crown just as he had immersed himself, and measure the water displaced. Readers may be interested to know that, according to Plutarch, the goldsmiths *had* cheated the king – the gold was mixed with silver.

In education, as we have suggested, heuristic models are used to aid instruction. We suggest story structures for children, and we provide children with algorithms for solving mathematical problems. The value and use of analogy, similes and metaphors is also widely recognized in contemporary learning theory. These are all heuristic devices. Various scientific investigative models have been applied in the past and their use in the classroom is commonplace. Heuristic models have been shown to be effective and have helped children in developing their understanding. Heuristic models can also be used to provide guidance for the educator in breaking down the processes of investigating or of designing and making into smaller, more manageable tasks. In exactly the same way heuristic design and technology problem solving models have been adopted to provide schema to inform our teaching of the subject. In the early years models such as these may be used to inform the teachers' scaffolding of the child's play. As a child's capabilities, in terms of symbolic representation, develop, their schemas will become more abstract and the child will be able to 'operationalize' their design for themselves and plan their own technology work.

In the early years much can therefore be accomplished by scaffolding the children's play. Fleer (1996) refers to the kind of scaffolding we suggest and argues that their use provides children with the opportunity to develop their own learning 'pathway'. She argues that space and time should be given to children so that they can enter into their own play scenarios while educators provide the learning framework to ensure that it is productive, citing Vygotsky (1978: 95–6) to argue that: 'The development from games with an overt imaginary situation and covert rules to games with overt rules and a covert imaginary situation outlines the evolution of children's play'.

Being a scientist: a game with rules

Figure 4.1. provides an heuristic model designed to support 'normal' scientific investigations. As previously suggested, the model provides what Bruner (1996) termed 'scaffolding' (see Chapter 2). It provides the teacher with a pathway that can be used to guide the children in their play and develop their capability. 'Normal science' was the kind of work for which the research teams led by Edison and Bell were famous. Their scientific research was closely associated with design problems and with invention. These kinds of normal scientific practices continue to take up most of the laboratory time in the adult world. They also provide the most appropriate basis for science education. The emphasis in normal science is on discipline and control. Scientific practice is also often considered to include a more creative form of 'revolutionary science' however (Kuhn, 1970). Revolutionary science serves to advance the *ways* in which scientists actually think about things. To be revolutionary in science a scientist therefore needs to have a very good understanding of the inadequacies of established knowledge. Such expectations are clearly inappropriate in elementary education. The heuristic model is labelled 'recipe number one' to emphasize that this is just one way of doing science. There are other legitimate ways of doing science but these do not concern us here.

It is important to note at this point that the process should not be applied so that some predetermined scientific knowledge (the 'understandings' identified above) are 'discovered' by the child, or for that matter, that they are simply tested. Even in primary schools, the limitations in terms of apparatus alone are such that any conclusive 'testing' of scientific theory is largely impractical. That is not the purpose of the experimental stage of the process at all. To take a rather obvious example, if it were felt

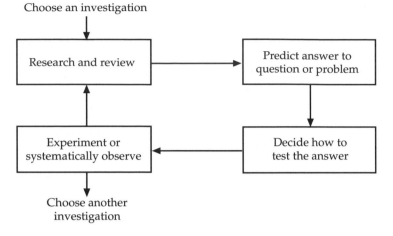

Figure 4.1 Being a scientist (recipe number one)

appropriate to teach a group of young children (that is, if they were to ask) what we know about the way things fall, we would want them to know that science tells us that, where two objects of very different weight have the same air resistance and they are dropped together, they will hit the ground together. This may be counter-intuitive but no practical experience that you might give the children or any demonstration that you could set up in a typical setting is likely to make the facts easier to accept. In this case the most appropriate means of introducing the children to the idea is by telling them the story of Galileo's famous demonstration where he dropped a cannon ball and a wooden ball of the same size from the Leaning Tower of Pisa. When we tell children how amazed the adult spectators were, we are legitimating the intuitive notion that heavy things drop faster and at the same time demonstrating the value of experiment and the authority of science over 'common sense'.

In the early years children require support in their investigations and we need to take care in selecting contexts that provide an appropriate basis for experimentation. In practice the biggest limitation in the early years is the form of measurement that is demanded. To use the specialist terminology, generally speaking, early investigations need to be developed to test the children's ideas about 'categoric variables' rather than 'continuous variables'. That means they need to work with different objects rather than being asked to measure differences between objects of the same kind. They might investigate which size or weight (i.e. the big or the little) car released to run down a slope travels the farthest but they would not be expected to test the same car given progressively heavier loads to carry down the slope. To take another example, different materials may be tested to find out if they float, but their weight and volume won't be considered at this stage.

The heuristic model shows four distinct stages in the process of investigation. The first of these is the 'research and review' phase where the children's existing knowledge of the subject is identified and developed. The particular problem or question that is to be investigated is clarified at this initial stage. At the second stage the children predict some the most likely answers to it. To take the example cited above, there are just two possibilities; either the big or the little car will go further. At stage three the children will usually require some help in deciding what evidence is needed to confirm (so far) or reject (outright) their prediction. In the case of the two cars it will be important for them to distinguish between a fair and a grossly unfair test; the cars will need to be released together at the same height. At stage four the appropriate data are collected and interpreted to decide whether there is sufficient evidence to accept the predicted answer and complete the investigation or enough doubt to take us back to the research and review stage and to consider some alternative answers or explanations. If the big car didn't travel so far, what could it be that slowed it down?

The 'long legs for jumping' and the 'ladybird' investigations cited in Chapter 1 provide further illustrations of the model in action. In the case of the ladybird hunt the children are supported in their systematic exploration and investigation of questions concerned with insect physiology (number of legs, spots etc.), the potential habitats (on leaves, on the ground, under rocks) and food sources (leaves, flowers, other insects). In the 'long legs for jumping' investigation an older, more experienced, group do some more structured experimentation using standard 'continuous' measurements.

Being a design technologist

As previously suggested, design and technology can also be seen as another game with rules. Figure 4.2 offers an heuristic model that is consistent with the National Curriculum orders for design and technology (DfE 1995a). Again it will be important for the teacher to make it clear to the children that this is just one recipe out of many for doing design and technology. Children should come to understand that there are countless other ways to solve problems, and that as they become more experienced they will develop their own strategies. In fact that is the whole purpose in introducing the heuristic in the first place, to help pupils develop their

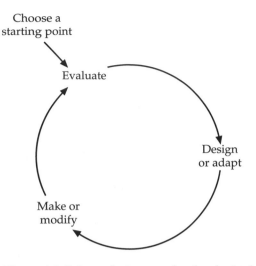

Figure 4.2 Being a designer and technologist (recipe number one)

confidence in successfully approaching designing and making problems to the degree to which they may generate their own schemas.

The heuristic model attempts to avoid the pitfalls of many previous attempts that have been made to define the designing and making process. The model identifies three distinct areas that determine children's capability in design and technology: designing, making and evaluating. The process is represented as a closed circle to emphasize the fact that any particular assignment may involve a number of cycles involving models and prototypes before a satisfactory solution is adopted. Further adaptation and modification is always a possibility. This approach can also be seen as consistent with the aforementioned APU's (1991) emphasis upon progressively more sophisticated interactions between the mind and the hand. A project involving children making 'ornaments for Mummy's dressing table' provides a very simple illustration of the model being followed. The school involved was fortunate in having a kiln and its use was timetabled throughout the year to allow each class an opportunity to use it. The 4 and 5-year-olds involved in the project had their turn in the spring term and the teacher decided to support the children in making Mother's Day presents. A range of household ornaments were brought into the classroom to be evaluated and each of the children was encouraged to tell us what they had at home. The teacher explained how they were going to make their own and asked the children to decide what kind of ornament their mother would like best. To encourage clear decisions to be made the children were asked to draw pictures of what they wanted to make. Figure 4.3 shows a

carla

I found it difficult   to
Make the Legs so   I Want to
change my design

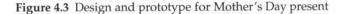

Figure 4.3 Design and prototype for Mother's Day present

typical design along with the 'photocopy' of an early prototype. The children were given stone coloured Plasticine to develop their designs and shown how to shape and finish it to their satisfaction. Their designs thus developed as they developed their own skills and evaluated their efforts. The teacher then 'photocopied'(yes photocopied!) the children's Plasticine prototypes to provide a record of the work. Finally the ornaments were shaped in clay, fired by the teacher and returned to the children, first for glazing and later to be wrapped in tissue, labelled as gifts and taken home to the delight of the parents.

A great deal can be achieved by children in the early years but the teacher needs to support and control the child's designing and technology work carefully. The curriculum should be highly scaffolded to ensure that the learning steps are not so steep as to allow the child to fail. The activities should also be matched to allow for different levels of capability, experience and awareness. Projects may be launched at any point from the secure framework of focused tasks concerned with either designing, making or evaluating. A few more examples are now provided to show what is required. In the first case the design and technology project lasted several weeks. It illustrates an approach that was applied with 4- and 5-year-olds in designing and making litter bins.

Designing and making litter bins

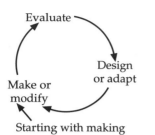

Starting with making

The 'litter bin' activity began with a focused whole (reception) class 'making' activity of the sort popularized by the *Blue Peter* TV programme. After a short discussion and introduction to the topic of litter, the 4-year-olds were given the task of constructing a litter bin from a prepared card (a net), which had been drawn on a sheet of A4 paper and then run through a photocopier loaded with light card (Figure 4.4). While the children sat on the carpet, they were provided not only with an example – 'the one I made earlier' – but also a demonstration of the construction process. The task was therefore highly supported and carefully matched to the children's (in this case limited) capabilities. The activity provided an opportunity to introduce a card construction convention to all of the children; that of cutting along bold lines and folding along dotted lines. The children were also shown how to fold the card along a ruler to get a sharp edge. A few children still needed individual support with their use of the scissors and the activity provided useful practice for them. The children were given the freedom to decorate their bins as they wished but at the end of the lesson all of the children had completed what was essentially the same product. They were told that they should take them home and that they were to discuss the design of the bins with their parents as the class was to evaluate them the next day. They were also asked to discuss where it was in their homes that litter was a problem and to look carefully at the design of the bins that they had. The children left school with a note to parents explaining what they were to do.

The children were proud of their bins, most significantly because they 'did something' – the lid swung backwards and forwards. Working from a shared design ensured that the teacher was able to control the use of materials carefully and ensure that all of the children were successful in their efforts. The parents were generally impressed by the skill that the children had demonstrated in constructing the model bins and rewarded them with praise and encouragement. This did not, however, detract from the evaluation the following afternoon, when the children easily identified

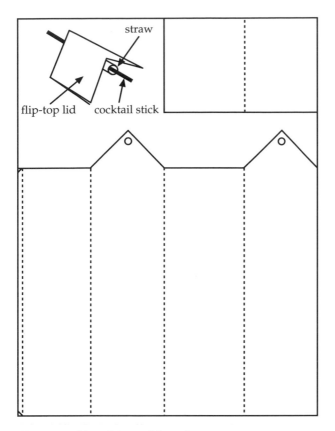

Figure 4.4 Litter bin card (a net)

the major design faults. It appeared that Mr Siraj-Blatchford's design was pretty awful really. The bin was too tall – it kept falling over. It was also very difficult to empty, and it was impossible to put a bag in it. The discussion generated a great number of ideas for improvement, and it was at this stage that the children's own designing activity was launched. Each child was first invited to think of a particular place in their homes where a litter bin was needed. They were then given the opportunity to draw their own design. Over the next week, with the teacher's support, sentences were added to the drawings describing their design and the teacher advised them on the use of suitable materials and methods. The making task was thereby differentiated and some of the more capable children were encouraged to make their models using a similar technique to the one initially introduced. Some adapted the original design, whereas others made up their bins using recycled boxes and cartons that had been collected especially for the purpose. The children then took their bins home overnight to show their parents, and in the subsequent evaluation session the best features of each bin were identified. Finally, the school's indoor litter collection needs were identified, and the children were set the task of designing and making a bin together in groups to satisfy that need.

The 'making' stage often provides the best starting point for designing and making because it gives the children the skills they require right at the beginning. It guarantees success while at the same time providing scope for adaptation and design improvements. Another example of a project starting with making might be in making greeting cards. The whole class could be taught how to make a new pop-up card mechanism. They could then adapt it to fit their specific purposes, determined to a large degree by the perceived interests and taste of the intended recipient.

Designing and making a yogurt product

Starting with evaluation

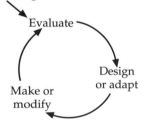

The evaluation stage can also serve as a starting point where children are more confident. Thus after a few pop-up mechanisms have been introduced, it may be enough just to show the children a range of new mechanisms. We are indebted to David Coates at Westminster College for one of our favourite (flavourite?) open-ended design and technology tasks with infants. This is first introduced by evaluating (tasting) various commercially made yogurt products. These may be savoury and/or dessert products and the relative merits, along with their television advertising, pricing and packaging are discussed. In evaluating the products the different ingredients are identified and the textures, colours and flavours discussed. This leads on to the production of yogurt in the classroom (supporting science) and the children's design of their own alternative food products with all the market research, packaging and display design work thrown in. In the process the children get to handle a wide variety of foodstuffs, colourings and flavourings. It is imperative to note, however, the use of food in infant design and technology is especially appropriate and rewarding but safety precautions must always be taken (see Appendix 6).

Designing a classroom for a rainforest

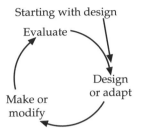

Starting with design

Evaluate

Make or modify

Design or adapt

Beginning at the design stage is, as previously noted, particularly demanding for young children. It is important to recognize that in these circumstances we are not just asking the children to design, we are actually expecting them to invent – and that is a lot harder. That said the following project shows that this can be successful where the children are particularly confident and capable.

A group of 5-year-olds were given the task to design a 'classroom for a

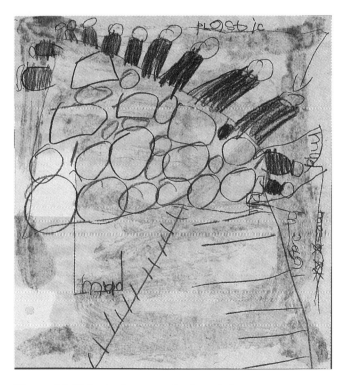

Figure 4.5 Helen's classroom in the rainforest

Box 4.1 The most productive starting points for science and design and technology activities are provided by the children themselves

Andrew, a 4-year-old, was sitting in the nursery sharing a book on dinosaurs with a student teacher. The teacher joined them and encouraged the child to talk about the dinosaurs: their skeletons and the shape and size of their footprints. He knew most of their names. The teacher asked if he knew what food the different dinosaurs ate. The child knew that certain dinosaurs ate others, that some ate meat and others ate plants. Asked how he identified which ate meat he identified those with 'big heads' – those having powerful jaws and teeth. As he looked through the book he named all the dinosaurs, some correctly and others with imaginative names to which he had added the suffix 'saurus'. He was seen later in the session playing in the outdoor sand pit making footprints and pretending to be a Tyrannosaurus rex.

---

rainforest'. This was part of an integrated topic that involved an extended consideration of classrooms and schooling. The children surveyed the layout of furniture in other classrooms; they also visited and took some lessons in 'role' in a Victorian classroom that was set up in a local museum. The children carried out a survey, and heard first-hand accounts of parents' and grandparents' experiences of their schools. They also planned classroom layouts and then reorganized their own classroom furniture to satisfy a variety of different needs.

Finally they were invited to design the 'classroom for the rainforest'. The initial stimulus was provided through a picture taken from an Oxfam calendar that showed children on their way to school in a small boat, carrying their books. A schools television programme had already introduced the notion of a rainforest. Sitting on the classroom carpet, the children discussed the climatic conditions with their teacher. They talked about what it was like when they got caught in heavy rain and they talked about fierce heat and sunshine. The children were asked to draw their ideas first and a variety of school and classroom designs were produced. The drawing and writing activity again provided an opportunity for the teacher and other children to intervene and support the task. When Helen shared her plan with the other children she explained how the room needed to be designed to allow plenty of air to circulate. One of the boys said, 'But with all of those tubes on the roof the children will get wet when it rains!' Helen smiled and told him, 'I already thought of that'. She held up her hand to operate an imaginary switch. 'The teacher would just flick a switch and they will all close down'. The designs were ultimately realized in a wide range of materials. The children were given time to try out their ideas with different materials and to make prototypes. These were evaluated collectively, again looking at the positive merits of different ideas. The children were given the opportunity to change and adapt their designs. The project was concluded with the usual (positive) evaluations.

Science for technology

In many projects we can construct three-dimensional models that can be tested before committing scarce materials to final assembly or production. The children's use of Plasticine before modeling clay in making the Mother's day ornaments was mentioned earlier. Such activities provide opportunities for investigations and may develop children's scientific expertise in the contexts of materials, structures, mechanisms or control. There are also possibilities here for introducing the relevant scientific explanations to children. An exploration of surface tension might thus pre-cede a designing and making assignment focused on producing a shelter from the rain. The children would then be able to apply their newly acquired knowledge that surface tension often acts as a skin and may stop water pushing through the tiny holes that are left in many woven fabrics. The treatment of this subject at this time will also provide an explanation for what might otherwise be seen later as the anomalous behaviour of these materials.

Layton (1993: 43) has referred to the desirability of children investi-gating questions such as 'Will this material serve for this purpose?' and 'Which of these materials is most suitable for this job?' Children might, for example, investigate thermal insulation, developing their scientific exper-tise in testing different materials to determine the relevant characteristics and then applying these principles to select the best available materials for the task in hand – making a winter coat for their favourite cuddly toy per-haps. In another project they might test water resistance, the strength of card or some other property of a range of materials in order to select those most suitable for their work. Many of these focused tasks will also provide a context in which other rich cross-curricular material may be presented.

Illustrative or investigative science activities may be employed to explain simple mechanisms and electrical circuits to children. Such activities will serve as a preliminary to setting designing and making assignments that encourage the children to develop their capability and apply their know-ledge for practical ends. Children can experiment with different joining techniques, testing for strength and durability. Different adhesives can be tested under controlled conditions. Experiments might also be conducted to test the viability of combining different ingredients in food products. Science contributes in many ways to technology and technology contributes to science; the products of children's designing and making can thus be tested and products can also be made for the express purpose of conducting scientific investigations. Children can make a wide variety of working models that lend themselves to further design and development and also to investigation. Balancing toys, musical instruments, periscopes and string telephones are all well within the capabilities of young children.

Throughout this book two sorts of design and technology activity have been referred to: directed or focused tasks and designing and making projects. Focused tasks often provide the children with the stimulus or the skills and knowledge that they need to successfully complete a designing and making project. While these terms have been drawn directly from the National Curriculum subject orders the Nuffield Design and Technology Project (1995) makes a similar distinction between resource tasks and capability tasks. It is important to remember here that, while it is usual to combine these two elements in design and technology, separate lessons can sometimes be planned for either. Implicit in our treatment of the subject is the fact that while a designing and making project without a focused task is probably undesirable, a focused task without a project may be more easily justified. Focused tasks without designing and making projects can stand on their own. In the context of the National Curriculum programmes of study for products and applications, in particular, it would be a mistake to rule out the possibility of this kind of focused study (DfE 1995a).

The heuristic models identified in this chapter provide the basis for planning, monitoring and assessing science and design and technology in nurseries and infant classrooms. The illustrations that we have provided demonstrate how a rich environment can be created in which children will be encouraged to explore, investigate and hypothesize, and to make, modify and use their own and other technological products. Much of the educators' success in developing this kind of environment will also depend upon their classroom organization: how they provide safe and well organized spaces, and how they store resources (see Appendix 5) so that they may be identified and accessed easily by the children.

The assessment of children's progress

One of the main purposes of assessment is to inform curriculum development. Profiles and records of achievement can also be used to provide records of progress; they may contain examples of drawings, paintings and written work. The child's development of process skills are more difficult to record and most design and technology work disappears at the end of the session when children take their projects home. Photographs can act as reminders for the child and an indicator of achievement and progress. In fact photographs are regularly used within many nursery settings as a means of assessment that has the added advantage of encouraging parental involvement in their child's learning. Parents love to see their child on a photograph, and are interested to find out the purposes of the activities that are depicted. In fact there are a number of ways photographs can be used to encourage learning in science and design and technology:

- looking at the camera itself and how it works;
- looking at negatives and photographs;
- taking photographs to record experimental findings;
- taking photographs for assessment purposes.

The effective teaching of science and design and technology in a large infant classroom or preschool setting is often very demanding. While pupils are working on their projects educators need to provide encouragement, questions, support with materials, help with modelling and making skills; they must also monitor quality and ensure safe practice. Whether all, or only some, children are engaged in science and design and technology at any one time, *all* of the children continually make demands upon the educator's time. The metaphor of spinning plates seems especially appropriate in describing the nature of the support task that is involved. Pupil interactions with the educator are typically very short and they need to be structured by a good understanding of progression within the subject. Specific guidance on this is provided in Chapters 5 and 6.

Making science, design and technology education more relevant to the child

Figure 5.1 'Experimental woodwork in the nursery: the two-year-old works at the bench beside his older brother' (Mellor 1953)

The National Curriculum and the new framework for the nursery curriculum for 4-year-olds has focused teachers' attention on the educational importance of science and design and technology (SCAA 1996). For many these subjects were previously considered little more than time fillers or 'fun' activities. Minibeasts was a 'good topic', and construction kits provided an appropriate occupation for children who had completed their 'real' work. Yet it would be a mistake to consider this work as something entirely new or as a subject more suited to older children. Edna Mellor, in her *Education Through Experience in the Infant School Years*, a book first published in 1950 when she was vice principal of the Manchester Training College, included the photograph shown in Figure 5.1 to illustrate appropriate practice (Mellor 1953). The caption below the picture reads: 'The two-year-old works at the bench beside his older brother' (1953: 43). Despite being published so long ago, the book shows images of girls working with saws, children engaged in large-scale construction using packing cases and making things with recycled materials. Science and design and technology have a long history in British preschool education. Mellor's (1953: 117) suggestions for early years science educators are worth quoting in full:

> It is necessary for the teacher herself [*sic*] to know the properties and possibilities of the materials which the children are handling, in order that she can answer their questions, remembering that they learn by words most readily when their questions are being answered. But her role is not just a passive one; she has an active and important part to play in leading children on to acquire further knowledge. She will draw their attention to phenomena such as frost on the window pane and dew on the grass, and lead their interest on as an alert and intelligent parent would do.

The best means of achieving appropriate, relevant and effective curriculum practice is therefore to provide a rich learning environment and to be aware of, and respond to, the educational potential of events and activities as they occur. As we have seen, the *Desirable Outcomes for Children's Learning* (SCAA 1996) indicate key goals for children by the time they enter compulsory education. Science and design and technology activities provide opportunities for supporting other areas of learning and in the following section we therefore provide guidance to identify these more fully.

Desirable outcomes and the National Curriculum

Science, design and technology activities provide contexts for integrated learning within each of the six 'areas of learning' that are defined in the desirable outcomes document (SCAA 1996) and in the following pages each area will be tackled separately. The areas are:

- Knowledge and understanding of the world;
- Creative development;
- Physical development;
- Language and literacy;
- Mathematics;
- Personal and social development.

Knowledge and understanding of the world

This area of learning, which most obviously includes historical, geographical and scientific strands, also covers design and technology. In fact, one of the stated aims of this area of learning is to provide a foundation for 'scientific and technological learning' (SCAA 1996). Children are thus expected to 'explore and select materials and equipment and use skills such as cutting, joining, folding and building for a variety of purposes' (SCAA 1996: 4).

Early years science and design and technology also has close links with both history and geography; the child's knowledge and understanding of their world will be aided by emphasizing these links. Early geography education begins with the local environment and early construction work offers the potential of modelling the local streets, pavements, shops, homes and transport systems. In fact environmental studies provide a very important context for curriculum integration in the early years. Having constructed the models the children may be given the opportunity in their play to plan, create and think about the needs and wants of the people in their community. Visits to the local market, to a supermarket, a canal, houses, streets, industrial sites or places of worship may be incorporated into a range of topics and enable children to build on their mental maps, to develop their spatial ability and think critically about their local environment and the wider world.

Young children will often show a sharp awareness of the purposes of some features of the area in which they live. They are often able to describe the things they see in the immediate environment of their home and some of the features of the built and natural environment that they have seen on the way to playgroup, nursery or school. Through exploring the 'made environment' children will have the opportunity to learn how their surroundings have been changed in response to people's needs. There are also opportunities here for addressing the needs of people with physical disabilities. One way of achieving this has been to encourage children to talk about their environment and how this meets their own needs and those of their family and other people they know. Access to buildings, events and public transport also provide useful environmental themes in the early years. Due to their size, children actually experience some of the same problems as the disabled. Raised platforms *could* be provided for them to view sporting and other public events yet they rarely are. Steps are often excessively steep and safety rails are inappropriately positioned. From a disability perspective, children may learn how new technological developments are not always beneficial to everyone, that there are often 'winners' and 'losers'. In a Scottish Development Education Centre (SDEC 1994) activity, children are provided with a picture showing a staircase leading to a public library. A number of people are shown experiencing difficulties on the staircase, one is elderly, another disabled, and a young mother is struggling with a pushchair. The children are then asked to imagine what the people might be thinking and they are asked to suggest how the access might be improved. The resource then suggests that the children be given the task of reviewing the adequacy of their school and its grounds from these perspectives. The children could then review local facilities more widely.

We can support children's development in this area of knowledge by encouraging children to explore and recognize features of made objects and to look closely at similarities and differences. Buildings relate to specific cultural, historical and geographical contexts. Focusing children's attention on buildings, and the spaces they create for different aspects of living, will help them to develop an awareness that technology has been used to meet the needs of individuals. Links between history and design and technology are strong and children's experience of these links are tangible. Past and present events in their own lives are often linked to toys and through photographs and cards associated with celebrations.

If the desirable outcomes are to be achieved children will need to be encouraged to talk about their observations, asking questions to gain information about why things happen and how things work; they should sometimes record their findings. This emphasis placed on talk runs through all the areas of learning. Science and design and technology provide an excellent medium for gaining confidence in speaking and listening. Many science and design and technology activities are also collaborative and provide opportunities for conversation and discussion. This is especially useful support for those children who have English as an additional language.

The SCAA desirable outcomes for knowledge and understanding of the world suggest that all children should have the opportunity to explore and select materials and equipment. There is, however, no indication of the range of materials and equipment to be used. In Chapter 6 more specific guidance will be provided in this respect.

Creative development

In terms of creative development the desirable outcomes focus on the development of children's imagination and their ability to communicate and express their ideas and feelings in creative ways. Music and art may be seen as key vehicles for enabling children to express these skills but design and technology has a significant part to play. Most three-dimensional work, such as 'box modelling', within a nursery setting is conducted as design technology, although it could often equally be seen as an art activity. A young child's imaginative response to the invitation to make something may take a wide range of three-dimensional forms. If the object is static it could be regarded as sculpture, whereas if it has a movable part it could be seen as technological simply because it includes a mechanism. The distinction becomes problematic when we consider kinetic art, however, and in practical terms it doesn't really matter; whatever the genre or intentions, the child is responding to a need and experimenting with techniques and materials. If however, skills and understanding are to be developed, it is important for the educator to recognize where such developments can be made. If a mechanism is intended as a means of allowing movement, this might be improved upon if it is made to respond to finer control. Similarly a sculpture may benefit from a different surface finish, a more stable base, or more effective joining.

In music, when playing an instrument or sound maker, the child is interacting with technology and may be considering the science of sound as well. Sound makers are often made in nursery settings but often with insufficient account being taken of design of the instrument. The child should be invited to consider how well it fits the hand and how well it serves its function. Equally, in the making process, investigation of the materials and the tools used to form them may often be explored more fully.

As previously suggested, children respond to what they see, hear, smell, touch and feel when they take part in food technology and the preparation of food and cookery have always been popular activities in preschool settings. They provide one of the few activities where all the senses can be fully utilized. Fantasy roleplay also provides opportunities for imaginative use of the senses in design and technology. Children are often extremely imaginative in their use of technological props. A visit to the hairdresser, a walk past a building site, the memory of a spaceship seen on television are examples of contexts that have prompted sustained imaginative play in nurseries. Individuals and groups have improvised, made and adapted resources for use in this play and they often demonstrate their understanding of the function of a wide range of technological products such as hairdryers, mechanical diggers and special clothing.

Physical development

As an area of learning, the desirable outcomes for physical development place an emphasis upon the development of physical control and manipulative skills. The document refers directly to the need for children to 'handle appropriate tools, objects, construction and malleable materials safely and with increased control' (SCAA 1996: 4). The contexts in which tools are used must be carefully planned and to help in planning activities the following guidance may be found useful:

• provide specific instruction on the correct use and care of tools;
• encourage an increasing degree of independence;
• introduce new materials that encourage the development of control.

We expand upon this advice in Chapter 6 when we consider progression. Further guidance on safety is also provided in Appendix 6.

Language and literacy

As previously noted, the conversations concerned with science and design and technology in which adults and children engage provide important opportunities for children to develop their speaking and listening skills. Children should be encouraged to talk about their work, to explain and extend their thoughts and ideas. A rich experiential curriculum will provide plentiful opportunities for children to ask questions to gain information about why things happen and how things work. The SCAA (1996) document suggests that children should talk about their experiences; the acts of designing, making, evaluating and observing and investigating provide excellent contexts for these discussions. Often these conversations will lead to opportunities for recording ideas in pictures and words (sometimes transcribed by an adult helper) for the benefit of parents and other audiences. As the National Curriculum suggests, children will soon develop competence and confidence in making things and 'they will use a growing vocabulary with increasing fluency to express thoughts and convey meaning to the listener' (SCAA 1996).

Stories, songs, nursery rhymes and poems and children's own made-up stories provide many opportunities for introducing or developing science investigations and design and technology projects. The children can:

- make props to accompany a story or nursery rhyme, e.g. making spiders for 'Anansi' stories or sound makers for 'Ride a cock horse';
- investigate questions that arise from discussing a story or rhyme; e.g. investigating spider habitats following a question concerning the rhyme 'Incy Wincy Spider'.

As suggested earlier, roleplay holds a central place in early learning. Children can make props or adapt existing materials to meet their needs in fantasy play. When we talk to the children about how things work, how things can be controlled and made to do what the child requires, they become more confident and improve their capability.

The *Desirable Outcomes* document (SCAA 1996) encourages preschool providers to help children to enjoy books, to handle them carefully and to understand how they are organized. This provides a further opportunity for design and technology because books are technological products themselves; they have been made and children can make their own. Treating books as made products, looking at the binding and the way the pages are held together will encourage children to treat the books with respect. Talking about the illustrations and the text and relating this to their printmaking, looking for the names of the printer, publisher, artist and binder will not only help their understanding of technology but also will help them to know that words and pictures carry meaning. Some excellent materials are available to support bookmaking in primary schools (see Appendix 2) and many of the techniques can be simplified and adapted for younger children. There is no reason why even the youngest children should not be involved in making books. Pictures and collages can also be made, pages sequenced and numbered, text added and, after simple binding, they can be used at home as well as in the setting. Encouraging children to use pictures, symbols, familiar words and letters to communicate meaning in their designing will show awareness of some of the different purposes of writing.

Mathematics

The desirable outcomes (SCAA 1996) for mathematics provide a foundation for numeracy. Science and design and technology provide contexts within which mathematical understanding can be fostered through practical activities and in using and understanding language in the development of simple mathematical ideas. Children can be encouraged to recognize and use mathematical language, describing shapes, positions, sizes and quantity when they are involved in the act of designing and making and investigation. When they select materials and when they try out their ideas with materials there are many opportunities to sort, compare, match, order, sequence and count. There are many chances for strengthening understanding of mathematics when designing and making. When using construction kits and making structures from wooden blocks there are many ways to make and repeat patterns. An element of design in structures is a recognition of the pattern that supports the stability of that structure. Regular use of construction kits will help children to recognize and recreate these functional patterns. In collaborative investigations, supported by the adult, the children will begin to use their developing mathematical understanding to show an awareness of number operations, such as addition and subtraction, and begin to use this language when solving practical problems.

Personal and social development

Scientists and other people who adopt a scientific approach demonstrate a particular set of personal and social skills. When someone claims to be a scientist, or to be adopting a scientific approach, what they are actually saying is that they are being systematic, rigorous, open minded, that they have a respect for evidence and alternative ideas. Scientists collaborate and their investigations draw upon a body of knowledge that has been accumulated by other members of the community of present and past scientists. In fact membership of this community is defined by the individual's commitment to the common procedures and practices of the scientific game. In much the same way, designers and technologists collaborate and learn from each other, they respect copy and patent rights and celebrate invention.

As we have suggested, when we introduce children to these practices we can use recipes that provide simplified models of scientific practice. They can play the scientist game or the design and technology game for themselves. These recipes are fine just as long as we don't follow them too slavishly and as long as we recognize that they don't constitute an adequate definition of science in themselves.

We encourage children to care for their environment and they are often enthusiastic recyclers, although this potential has barely been tapped in Britain. Children are also often acutely conscious of and concerned about fairness and injustice and this provides a wonderful opportunity to involve them in local campaigns. These may be associated with issues of direct concern to the children themselves, such as road crossing or a local play area, or of concern to their parents. Children have often benefited from being involved in campaigns to develop or to save their preschool setting itself from closure.

When children make a statement about a designed product, such as a toy, or they exhibit a preference for a particular type or brand of clothing they exhibit their use of self-selected criteria for making judgements. Choices and preferences relate to values and value judgements. This is an important developmental strand within design and technology. Consideration may initially be given to likes and dislikes at what may be considered a superficial level. But even at this early age children are beginning to be aware of values within design and technology, and this may be encouraged by introducing issues like the need to conserve and not to waste materials. We can introduce criteria for the selection of suitable materials. We can also begin to discuss issues of 'fairness' and equity.

The things that children design and make are products and they are designed and made for particular purposes and users. Children can be encouraged to develop sensitivity to the needs and feelings of others through design and technology activities. We can even contribute to multicultural education by fostering respect for people of other cultures and beliefs. When we encourage children to make products for use by adults in the local community or other children in their play, we encourage them to think about the needs and preferences of other people. We have used all of the following examples in our own work;

- making toys (e.g. mobiles) for baby brothers and sisters and bookmarks for a local home for the elderly;
- making a card designed specifically for one particular person, rather than assembling ready-made components; this encourages sensitivity to the needs and feelings of others;
- designing and making Eid and Diwali cards to celebrate these festivals as well as Easter and Christmas;
- preparing and sharing food associated with a cultural or religious festival encourages respect for people with other cultures or beliefs.

Science and design and technology may also play a major role in cultivating a sense of wonder about the world. In recent years, anxiety has been expressed about the growing gender polarization of concern regarding issues such as environmental pollution and bio-diversity. While the association of women with nature and men with science and technology has been emphasized by some feminists, this may only serve to reinforce popular stereotypes. In our opinion, however, there can be little doubt that male values do require some redefinition. If we are to achieve a peaceful and sustainable future, then we must begin to prioritize cooperation, caring and social interaction over competition, aggression and individualism. Given the degree of cultural contamination in this respect, some emphasis upon the development of a sense of wonder about nature and the environment may be seen as especially important for boys (Siraj-Blatchford and Patel 1995).

Creating a rich learning environment

One of the most important ways that we can make science and design and technology relevant to children is by giving them the time and free access to the tools, instruments and materials that they require to investigate, design and make for themselves. This involves managing time and managing space. If we want to encourage children to take a closer look at an insect discovered in their play, then we need to make sure they know where to find a magnifying glass. Similarly, if we want them to create their own props for play, improvising a camera for example, for use on their fantasy holiday, they need to have access to the boxes, cardboard tubes and adhesives necessary for its construction.

Ideally we want to develop a safe and well-organized space that could be used for a wide variety of purposes and develop systems for the storage of all of our instruments, tools and materials so that they are easily accessed by the children. The problem is, of course, that it will be impossible to store all of the resources that you will want to use throughout the year in one teaching area. Most settings therefore consider it essential that work is organized under broad themes and topics.

Often the same area in a room is used for all practical 'craft' activities. This is an effective solution as it confines messy work within one area and makes for easier cleaning. Materials and tools can also be stored in the area, which will allow children ready access to the things they will need in their making. However, if children's experience of design and technology is to be extended we need to consider the effect that space has on the type of work in which the children engage. Different design and technology activities may require us to consider how to allocate space in more imaginative ways. Always confining activities to one area may impose restrictions on the type of product made. Use of an outdoor area for example does appear to encourage children to tackle making things differently. Collaborative work is also far easier to manage when there is adequate space.

If more imaginative use is to be made of space it is important not only to plan for the expected response but to try and predict what may happen unexpectedly. Taking design and technology work out of the usual physical context often has surprising results. Work may be extended in time as well as space and more children than usual may become involved in the process, joining, participating, taking a break and then rejoining the activity as the work progresses. The result of such work may be a child-designed roleplay area. Obviously this has implications for the use of space and the need to plan such activities demands effective day-to-day management and collaborative planning.

When choosing the best place for a design and technology table or area consider the following:

- *Location*
  Is the table in a location where there will be few distractions? Avoid placing a worktable near doorways, other thoroughfares, or next to windows. Some children become easily distracted and the safe use of tools, whether they be scissors, a hole punch or a saw, requires concentration.

- *Timing*
  Will children have time to work in a sustained way or will their activity have to be curtailed because the work area is required for some other purpose at a specific time?

- *Purpose*
  Are links being made between design and technology work and other areas of the curriculum? Is this on a regular basis or does the linkage occur when it relates to certain themes? Changing the working layout often stimulates connections that would not normally occur. For example, placing hole punches, paper and treasury tags next to the writing area has been used to stimulate children to make books. Card boxes, tubes, string and tape placed in an imaginative play area have been used by children to make 'power packs' for use in their play. Construction kits may be used alongside more conventional resources to teach sequencing skills.

- *Scale*
  Will work be large scale or small scale, individual or collaborative? How can space be used to encourage particular ways of working?

Planning the resource base

Space to store consumable resources is a problem for many providers. Careful selection of recyclable materials is the key to effective management. Too often providers accept bags full of random selections of recyclable materials without any consideration of their value for children's learning. A huge box full of odds and ends does little to enhance a child's understanding of design and technology – or any other aspect of learning. This pile of junk may be translated into a system of sorted sheet materials for making quality products at little cost. Organizing materials in this way will allow children to select materials more easily. They and their parents will see that they are not filling in time making 'junk' models. Take a large sturdy box and subdivide it with other boxes. Specific materials can be requested of parents when stocks are reduced.

Storage of materials and tools

There are several important issues in considering methods of storage of materials and tools. These include: safety problems, supporting children's independence, effective management of space and financial concerns. These considerations have an impact upon both the provision for teaching design and technology and the quality of children's work. Before addressing specific means of storage it is as well to make an audit of the storage requirements of the setting. As each setting will have specific as well as general requirements the following comments should act as an aide mémoire rather than a definitive list.

Access
- Is access to materials and tools open or restricted? What criteria are used for this decision?
- Access to some tools may need to be restricted for safety reasons – for whom and why?
- Are materials and tools out of the way but accessible when required? How does this affect children's experiences of design and technology?

Space
- We often store too many things. Does forward planning indicate when specific resources are likely to be needed?
- Are parents encouraged to contribute to the effective organization of resource storage? Parents can be encouraged to 'undo' and collapse boxes with their children, to look at box cards (nets) and notice what information is printed on the box etc. As well as permitting boxes to be stored more easily children will also extend their understanding of design technology, mathematics and language and literacy in the process.

Safety
- Decisions have to be made about which tools are to be on open access to children and which should be stored out of reach. Those tools that are used regularly, such as hole punches and snips can be stored on a board. Drills, saws and reamers, see page 97, should be kept out of reach to be used only under supervision.
- What systems are there for teaching newly admitted children about tools and equipment?

- Are tools stored in a way that encourages respect and care for equipment? Scissors and snips stored on silhouettes, hooks or in a block rather than stacked in a tin will encourage better care for the tools as well as providing a quick visual check for missing items. Tapered reamers should be stored in a box in the staff cupboard and used only under supervision. Some staff protect the end of the reamer with a cork when it is not in use.

In some settings, where child-elected activities are the main means of learning, the management of equipment is especially crucial to the quality of experience for the child. Ready access to a carefully controlled range of equipment will encourage development of skills and ideas, knowledge and understanding. Consider the following as starting points.

Managing the use of construction kits

Do the children have ready access to a limited, changing range of construction kits or are the same ones always available? Are kit components, the pieces, kept in one large box or in smaller boxes within that box for ease of access and sorting? Do the children know where to find things – and where to return them? For example, an actual component, such as a piece of Duplo, or picture of item can be attached to the box or drawer. Blocks can be stored on silhouettes of the shaped items painted on shelves at a height accessible to children.

Managing textiles

As with other materials, a storage box for textiles is an effective means of managing children's use of a range of materials. It may not, however, be in use every day. If it is stored under a table at the side of the room it may still be visible to children and accessible if required. Longer lengths of fabric can be wrapped around a cardboard tube. Kitchen roll tubes are an appropriate size as they can easily fit into a cardboard box. They are also of a manageable size for children to handle. Smaller pieces of fabric are best stored in plastic storage containers; large sweet jars are particularly useful.

Managing tools

Scissors, snips and single hole punches may be used in several areas of the room. In the writing area they may be used when making books. They may also be used by another group of children to make their own shoe lacing boards and by another group box modelling. The use of hole punches can therefore be managed more effectively by storing them centrally on a surface – perhaps a shelf or table that has silhouettes, hooks or a block for each tool. They are then accessible for use throughout the setting. Hole punches are small and can easily be mislaid, casting an eye on the silhouettes at the end of a session is a quick means of checking for their return.

Managing 'consumables'

Storage boxes with small drawers are available quite cheaply from DIY stores. They are ideal for storing small items such as paper fasteners and treasury tags, paper binders and washers. Elastic bands stretched around the box will hold the drawers in place. Items can be decanted from this central storage system as required. An effective storage system for use on the working table can also be adapted from plastic containers that have a number of sections; containers used for savoury dips are especially useful. The provider can control the context of learning by putting out selected items or by restricting the range of items stored in the box. It is important to present children with a comprehensive range of items rather than piles of very similar materials. This encourages purposeful working. It is also more cost-effective to put out a wide range of a small number of fixings and fasteners rather than many of the same item. Alternatively, a purpose-made storage container for small items can be made quite easily from large matchboxes.

Managing graphics materials

An effective way of storing paper is to use apple boxes. They are sturdy and stack easily. They can be sprayed with different colours of aerosol paint to differentiate the types of paper stored. A range of papers – newspaper, brown paper, drawing paper, coloured paper – can then be cut to size to fit the boxes. This allows the children to select paper and to develop an understanding of their particular qualities. A large block of wood can be drilled with holes slightly larger in size than a pencil. A range of pencils can be stored in this way (HB, 2B, 6B). Children can then learn to select pencils according to their preferences. A similar method may be used to store felt tipped markers. The tops of the pens can be glued firmly into the drilled holes.

   In this chapter we have shown how science and design and technology educational activities can be helpful in encouraging progress in the desirable outcomes of learning (SCAA 1996). Specific advice has been given on how to create the sort of rich learning environment within which an appropriate, relevant and effective curriculum practice may be achieved.

6

Practical support for progression and continuity

The approach that we take in defining progression and in supporting the development of schemes of work that will ensure continuity is based upon the notion of scaffolding. In Chapter 2 we cited Smith (1994) who identifies three aspects:

1 where the teacher may direct the child's attention to different aspects of a situation;
2 where the child is helped to break down a task into a sequence of smaller tasks which are more manageable;
3 where the teacher helps the child to sequence the steps in the right order.

Our approach to the first of these aspects has been to encourage educators to enter into discussion and informed engagement with the child. The heuristic models provided in Chapter 4 are intended to satisfy the second aspect of scaffolding and this chapter will offer guidance in the third crucial area. If we are to sequence the steps effectively we need to know in what order they should come. Put another way, we need to understand what it is that defines progression in science and design and technology. In providing the following advice we have taken account of the early development of children's capabilities that we have noted in our own experience. The principles that we base our guidance upon are related to 10 areas of capability:

In design and technology education:
1 designing;
2 the use of materials;
3 using tools to make holes;
4 use of cutting tools;
5 joining, fixing and making mechanisms;
6 building structures;
7 evaluating products and applications.

In science education:
8 asking questions;
9 experimenting and exploring;
   • using instruments;
   • measuring;
10 developing a knowledge and understanding of science.

There are many different ways of approaching the education of young children. A setting may, for example, reflect a particular philosophical tradition such as Montessori (1912) or Steiner (1968), or it may follow an approach that advocates free-flow play. In most settings, however, activities related to science and designing and making play some part in the educational programme. Children often find making something an enjoyable experience and they approach it with confidence, but for many children this enjoyable experience may remain just that and nothing more. When we start to unpack what it is that the child is learning in the activity we can plan to extend such experiences and we can plan for learning. The early years of a child's life are a time of rapid development. It is a period when most children will demonstrate a capacity for learning at a speed that may never again be reached in later life. This is why good patterns of extended, planned learning are so necessary if a child's true potential is to be realized.

Planning for learning in both science and design technology contains similar key elements; these relate to developing physical, manipulative skills, acquisition of knowledge through practical experiences and developing questioning approaches. We could say that these are the basic principles for any planned scheme of progression. Confidence is also an important aspect to consider when planning for progression. We know, from our own educational experiences, that we enjoy learning when we can see our achievements, when we can make things happen, when we have control and, most importantly, when we have gained confidence in our ability. Confidence is perhaps the key to learning, yet we also need to take risks, to try out new techniques, try new materials and express new ideas. This inevitably means that, at times, things won't work out as expected, but if we have gained confidence from being successful in the past we view this as just another part of the learning process, we accept the occasional failure and learn from it. This is why scaffolding or success management is so important.

Adults often underestimate the capacity that children have for learning, and for drawing conclusions about science and technology in the world around them. Our argument has been that we should start with children's experiences and interests, adopting an approach that responds to the learning needs of the child through a developmentally appropriate curriculum.

Designing

As we scaffold or structure activities using the designing, making and evaluating model, we encourage the children to be designers and technologists, and to think about the reasons for their making activity. We also encourage them to plan their work and to review their progress as they go along. Good practice demands that children do a lot more thinking than is often expected of them. As far as possible they need to make their own decisions rather than simply follow directions or assemble prepared materials. In essence they need to be supported and taught to make informed decisions. It is not enough to allow children to explore or to play aimlessly with tools and materials. Limited, low level activities may lead to frustration and restrict development; and inappropriate use of tools and equipment may also result in injury. Appropriate support is therefore essential in order to help children to develop an independent approach to design and technology activity.

In terms of design, schemes should be developed to ensure that children enjoy a good deal of early success and gain confidence in their designing and making before being set demanding tasks or problems to solve. A good deal of the design should at first be provided by the adult, allowing the child to adapt it to their own purposes. Designs should be evaluated and the child encouraged to always look for the positive qualities of a design that they may be able to incorporate into their own.

Use of materials

Malleable materials are commonly used in preschool settings. A scheme for progressively extending children's skills might begin with dry sand, moving on to damp sand, to playdough, plastic/wet clay; bread dough; Plasticine; papier mâché.

Manipulation of materials may also be extended with sheet materials, card and paper. Planning opportunities for progression of materials will encourage the development of a stronger grip and application of pressure appropriate to the child's physical development. We can show how paper can be scrunched, crumpled and folded to achieve different effects. This may occur naturally in play; wrapping things in paper or making an 'envelope'. Manipulating card may be best achieved through using card tubes such as those that are used as a core for kitchen roll or gift wrapping paper. Printing is an activity that is popular in play groups and nurseries; the implements that are used for this are often objects such as cotton reels, sticks or sponges. To develop manipulative skills children can easily make their own blocks from card tube. Kitchen roll tubes can be cut to a size to fit the hand. The tube can be pushed into a shape and the shape retained with masking tape. These printing blocks can then be used on paper, fabric or kitchen roll. With appropriate support, the children will be able to develop their spatial awareness when organizing the patterns they print. Sequencing shapes and colours is a natural development of this activity. The products made may serve a variety of purposes, for example, drapes for roleplay, wrapping paper or background display paper.

When printing children will explore the qualities of the surface of the material, be it paper, card or fabric and they will see how the colour is absorbed – how it runs or stays on the surface. The decoration of fabric can be achieved in other ways, using fabric markers, crayons or paints. This should not be seen as simply a matter of making marks. Progression may be encouraged by presenting children with a range of markers, crayons, pastels and paints and a range of fabrics to work on. The quality of marks will be influenced by the composition of the fibres.

Colour, colour blending and absorbency are investigated in the dyeing process. Tie-dye is a messy process with young children. Dip-dyeing is a better alternative but equally effective process. Two sheets of plain, strong kitchen roll can be pleated and retained with pipe cleaners and clothes pegs. The paper can then be quickly dipped into bowls of dye – a sequence of yellow, red and blue are very effective – changing the angle of the dip for each colour. Plenty of newspaper is needed on surfaces (another science teaching point). The paper is then untied and opened out to be left to dry.

Fabrics, threads, yarns, and trimmings are often used as materials for collage. Making collage with small pieces of fabric provides an opportunity to learn that materials have different properties. An opportunity is provided for exploring sensory perceptions; feeling and smelling the fabrics and seeing how the glue soaks through some fabrics and not others.

Box 6.1 Clothes for teddy

My 4-year-old daughter decided to make some clothes for her teddy. Unbeknown to us she took some of her mother's fabric (it was best silk that she had discovered in a drawer). After we had discovered the finished article and recovered from the shock we asked how she had made it. She made the pattern for the shirt by putting the fabric on the floor (carpeted!). She told us that she had put the teddy on top and cut around the body. She used that first piece as a template and had then sewn them together. She had watched her mother sewing before and was always cutting . . . making small props for her play. I don't know what I would have felt about her making the shirt if I had known she was going to do it on the carpet – or with the best silk !

Key teaching points are:

- teach children to recognize a wide range of natural and manufactured materials;
- show the importance of each material in everyday life;
- provide opportunities for children to explore the qualities and characteristics of each of the different materials.

It is important to observe how individual children manipulate and use resistant materials. There seem to be no general rules defining progression; it is simply a matter of providing for individual needs. It will be found that some children, contrary to our expectations, can handle some 'difficult' materials more easily than others. Materials need to be matched to individual capabilities, providing a degree of challenge while ensuring successful outcomes. When materials are to be joined, some children find plastic bottles, cut into sections, easier to punch holes into than thin card boxes. Greater pressure is often required to punch a hole in card. Some children also find card tubes, especially kitchen roll or gift wrap tubes, easier to hold and manipulate than a box. The tubes can therefore be cut to size with greater accuracy. These cylindrical shapes lend themselves to the making of snakes, caterpillars and articulated parts of bodies of puppets, such as arms or legs. Where large boxes are to be used for large scale modelling work it is worth preparing the boxes by dismantling them and putting them back together inside out. They can then be painted without inevitable black print showing through.

Apart from the usual recycled boxes, cartons and containers, the sheet materials and recycled textiles, a supply of wood will be valuable. Technology Teaching Systems (TTS) (see Appendix 5) supply packs of 590 mm length, 8 mm square and 25 mm × 5 mm section wood that will serve most purposes. We have also found the TTS 5 mm dowel (wooden rod) packs and their wooden wheels useful. Where budgets are tight you can make your own wheels by sandwiching cardboard with PVA glue between thin card wheels. You will find a lot of other ideas in the TTS catalogue and should consider providing a supply of cotton reels, pipe insulation and tap washers to be used with the dowel as a simple means to get children's models moving.

Tools for making holes

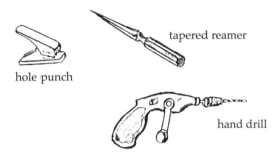

Figure 6.1 Tools for making holes

We have found that the hole punch constitutes an essential first tool for children in design and technology. As soon as the child is able to make a hole in something they are able to join it onto something else. Any double hole or small single hole punch, of the type used in offices, will do; the plastic base should be removed and the tool used upside down as this allows the user to see where the hole will be positioned. Having introduced the tool and shown the children how to use it, the educator can then plan progressively more difficult and physically demanding making activities that require holes. Designs that demand holes in progressively more resistant materials such as plastic and card can be introduced. The educator is therefore able to respond to the child's developing manipulative skills and the physical capability. A typical sequence of materials might involve the child progressing from: thin paper to thick paper; from thin card to card tubes; from thin plastic bottles to thicker card; from yogurt pots to thick plastic bottles.

The range of size of hole and the positioning of holes is very limited with a hole punch. To extend this skill, and to follow children's interests, holes should be made with other tools. For larger scale work and for extending skills in controlling the size and position of holes a tapered reamer is essential. This is a tool that is now used in many early years settings. As can be seen from the illustration above it has the appearance of a screwdriver but has a tapered point. The blades are enclosed and cutting is achieved by twisting, rotating and pushing the tool rather than cutting. People often use pencils or scissors to make holes, but this is potentially dangerous; the reamer is a much safer and a more appropriate tool for the task. Using a tapered reamer is the most effective – and the safest – method of making a hole in a thick box or plastic bottle but it is a tool that must be used under supervision. When using the reamer ensure that the material in which the hole is to be made is held securely on a firm surface.

Progression is achieved quite simply with the reamer. It may be modified to make holes of different size by wrapping masking tape around the blade. Making holes of different sizes by this method allows for a wide range of possibilities. A small hole in a bottle will allow card tubes to be attached, for example when making a puppet. Large holes may be made in shoe boxes. These can then be connected with plastic nuts and bolts to make large scale robot-like movable figures. Packing boxes can also be joined in this way; this provides a particularly useful method of putting together boxes for large scale construction work.

As indicated earlier, the child's confidence with tools can be encouraged by gradually extending the range of materials on offer. A suitable progression of materials for use with the tapered reamer would be: thin card (cereal) boxes to card tubes (kitchen roll or gift wrap tubes), to thicker card boxes (packing boxes).

The pistol grip hand drill is light and well balanced and has been used successfully with young children. Again the most important thing to

---

Box 6.2 Making 'rain makers'

Measure along a cardboard tube at regular intervals and mark these with elastic bands, holes can then be made with the reamer through which straws may be inserted. These can be held in place with masking tape. (Other materials suitable for different age groups could be used. Dowel could be sawn to length, inserted and held in place with a dab of PVA or glue from a glue gun. Pipe cleaners could be used and held in place with paper tape.) The tube could then be filled with materials such as grit, small pebbles, rice or balls of tin foil. The length, diameter, thickness of the tube, the type of materials used for the 'stick' as well as the contents will alter the sound. The ends of the tube may be covered with several layers of pasted newspaper to make a drum head and therefore another way of making and controlling sound.

remember is that the material to be drilled needs to be held securely. In fact this applies to cutting tools as well; the best way to ensure that it happens is to make a simple rule that is rigorously applied: 'You mustn't use the drill or the saw unless the thing that you are cutting is held by a G clamp or the vice'. Another rule that you should apply to both tools right from the start is, 'Always cut away from yourself'. As the children develop their capability and confidence in using the tools the use of a bench hook can be introduced as an alternative means of holding materials securely.

TTS supply two sizes of drill bit that we have found adequate for most purposes. One provides for a push fit to 5mm dowel and the other will produce a hole that will allow 5mm dowel to run freely. To simplify things, we have found it convenient to restrict the supply of dowel to this 5mm size in the early years and to have two different colour drills each fitted permanently with these different size drill bits.

Cutting tools

In most nurseries a good deal of emphasis is placed on children acquiring cutting skills. To this end children are given opportunities to use scissors. Careful matching of materials to tools is as important with scissors as with any other tool. If a variety of papers, of different thickness and texture, are provided the children are more likely to develop an understanding of the particular qualities of both the materials and the tool. Thicker materials such as card and plastic are often difficult for young children to cut effectively with scissors.

Safety snips are spring loaded and therefore allow the child to cut a var-

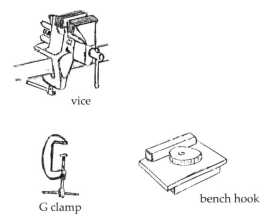

vice

G clamp

bench hook

Figure 6.2 Holding materials securely

iety of materials more readily than scissors. Card and plastic can be cut without hurting fingers in the way scissors do when applying pressure. Snips can also be used in either hand. We should provide children with the opportunity for making things with an increasingly broad range of materials and this can be matched by introducing new and more complex tools. Cutting paper with scissors will lead to cutting card or plastic with snips and then to cutting card tubes and thin wood with a saw.

The key teaching points should be:

- matching the appropriate tool to the materials – for effective use. This involves developing an understanding of why the tool works, which parts cut and how this can be controlled;
- matching the appropriate tool to the materials – for safe use. This involves developing an understanding of the particular qualities of the materials, for example, soft or hard;
- matching the appropriate tool to the materials – for quality. This involves matching the tool to the material to meet the child's own expectations and needs, in particular its suitability to meet its intended purpose.

Joining, fixing and making mechanisms

Even in the earliest stages of designing and making the child will want to join things together to allow movement or to fix them securely. The first means of achieving this are usually provided by PVA glue and masking tape, which is easy to cut and can be painted, thus making it infinitely superior to Sellotape for these purposes. It is important that children should learn how to select the appropriate method of fastening for themselves. Initially they will need a good deal of reminding about the advantages and disadvantages of the alternatives. PVA glue is particularly useful for attaching small pieces of paper or fabric to wood, plastic or card tubes and for fastening wood to wood. It should be applied thinly but

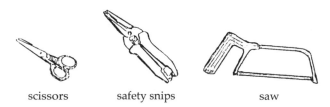

scissors   safety snips   saw

Figure 6.3 Cutting tools

Boxes can be cut in such a way that an integral hinge is formed. This may be controlled with fingers, hand or artstraw.

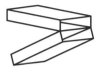

Treasury tags may be used to restrict movement as well as to control it.

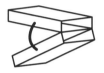

Figure 6.4 Box hinges

children won't discover this for themselves; at first this needs to be demonstrated. Clipping materials together with a clothes peg or paper clip will help to hold them in place until the glue dries.

Low tack masking tape, on which the adhesive is not strong, should not damage a model if a child decides to take it apart. Brown paper tape provides an alternative and is an effective way of joining boxes and tubes. It presents a hazard if torn however; it really needs to be cut with scissors. It is also as well to remember to use a damp sponge to wet the tape; the taste is horrible! Tape can be used to create hinges or to join boxes or tubes to allow movement.

As soon as the child is able to make a hole in a material, a wide range of much more sophisticated joining and fixing possibilities is opened up. We have found the following list of fixings and fasteners specially useful when introduced in sequence: long treasury tags; large paper binders; shorter treasury tags; large paper fasteners; short treasury tags; short paper binders and fasteners; elastic treasury tags; pipe cleaners; string.

Treasury tags

Treasury tags come in a wide variety of sizes. Longer ones are ideal for lacing together large sheets of card or boxes to make 'dens' or hinged doors. Short ones fit through tubes or small boxes easily. For young children who cannot yet tie a knot, treasury tags are a rapid and effective way of joining

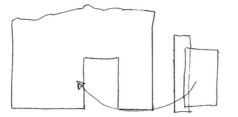

This system is also useful for joining boxes or tubes to allow for movement.

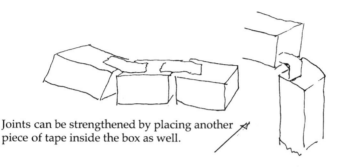

Joints can be strengthened by placing another piece of tape inside the box as well.

Figure 6.5 Tape hinges

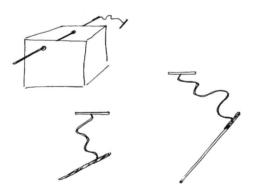

Figure 6.6 Treasury tag 'needles'

things together. They also provide a very adaptable temporary fastening as they come in a variety of lengths. Some children may find it difficult to grip the end of the tag. This problem may be eased by making a 'needle'; this may be achieved by wrapping a piece of masking tape around to form a

Box 6.3 Joining textile materials

We were preparing for a celebration related to Haile Selassie, of particular importance to some of the nursery children, and were discussing music and costumes. The celebrations included drumming initiated by one parent and wearing costumes made by the children. As can be seen from the photograph, the children made their own costumes rather than assembling ones made by adults. One child even produced a drawn design for her costume which closely matched the finished product. The fabric used was felt that had been used for shop display purposes. Holes that had appeared were usefully enlarged for a head or an arm. Some of the different coloured felts were joined with a stapler, which provided a speedy and practical method of joining. These children had not yet been introduced to sewing with a needle and thread. Most of the joining was achieved by punching holes in the felt and using treasury tags to lace the garment together – this also had the advantage that they could be unlaced and taken off. The activity promoted collaborative work between the children and the role of staff became that of 'aides'. The children had to describe every action they wished the staff to help them with – they acted as instructors. The satisfaction of producing work of this quality was very evident.

Figure 6.7 Children making costumes

Box 6.4 Using treasury tags

Charlene had just moved into the reception class and the class were making 'shooters' for the Hindu festival Holi. (Coloured powder should really be used but it was decided that tissue paper was cleaner!) Her design and technology experience in the nursery had enabled her to match tools to materials and had given her the confidence to try out her own ideas. The shooter was made from two tubes, the longer one fitting snugly inside the other so that it could move up and down. Holes were made in the ends of both tubes but for the shooter to work they needed to be joined in some way. Joining the tubes to allow for movement proved a problem, however. First she tried string but couldn't tie it, so she attached the ends with masking tape, but this didn't allow for movement. Next pipe cleaners and string treasury tags were tried, but without much success. Then she found an elastic treasury tag from some packaging used to hold plastic hair slides in place. This was the answer. Treasury tags may be used to restrict movement as well as to control it . She had discovered a way of joining the tubes to make a shooter for Holi which had effective movement based on stored energy. A good deal of experimentation then took place to find ways of preventing the tissue from falling out of the bottom of the tubes. After persevering with masking tape, a solution was found.

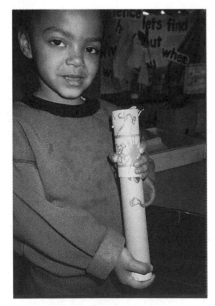

Figure 6.8 Holi shooter

A friend held the outer tube and pushed up the inner tube to allow masking tape to be attached to the inner tube without restricting any movement. Other children were soon copying the 'invention' and given personal tuition by this young teacher.

Another outcome of this work was that the length of the treasury tag was found to produce different results in the ways in which the inner tube could be pushed up and rotated. This technique has been built on by other children to make puppets with heads that pop up such as 'animals that live in holes'.

longer point. Threading a treasury tag through holes opposite each other in a tube or box is made easier by attaching a straw to the tag end.

Paper fasteners

Paper fasteners are very useful in developing children's skills in manipulating and controlling movement. They come in a variety of sizes and can be obtained from most office suppliers. They may be used for fastening card, paper, plastic and some fabrics. Care should be taken when buying paper fasteners that the head of the fastener is larger than the hole made by a hole punch.

Paper binders

These are simply larger versions of paper fasteners. They have a wider head, which means that heavier card can be joined and the paper binder will not fall out of the hole. Most paper binders come with washers. These are useful as spacers. When placed between layers of card they allow freer movement.

Pipe cleaners and garden wire

Pushed through two holes and twisted, a pipe cleaner makes a very good temporary fastener. The metal wire in the pipe cleaner will retain shape and the chenille covering will absorb paint, thus also making a good printing implement. Where large boxes need to be joined to make play environments or large scale props and models, adults may use garden wire in the same way. Sharp ends can be covered in masking table to avoid injury.

Box 6.5 Making a robot

A child in one nursery wanted to make a robot, one that would move. When the types of movement were discussed it was determined that there had to be vertical and horizontal movement. This was tried out using shoe boxes. Holes were made in the boxes (a tapered reamer was the safest tool for the job) and nuts and bolts taken from a construction kit were used to join the boxes to gain the desired effect. One of the important features of this process was that the ideas could be tried out without having the restriction of using preformed construction kit parts; the boxes could be easily modified. The mechanisms of the robot – the moving parts – were also made and modified before it was decorated.

String

Although this is a very useful fastening it does pose special problems for children who are still developing their skills in knot tying. A technique discovered by children and which we often use is to thread string through a hole and then secure the end with masking tape.

Often there are insufficient components in a construction kit to make large scale models. But plastic nuts and bolts can also be used with recyclable materials.

Children are very adept at trying out ideas, making modifications and evaluating their effectiveness if they are allowed time and provided with effective support. This is often demonstrated when children are shown a basic technique or idea that captures their imagination. We have found that making snakes and caterpillars from tubes provides a means of encouraging children to develop their skills in making holes and using connectors. When joining tubes, greater movement can be achieved by squashing the tube and cutting off the corners. Children have found that the angle of the cut and the positioning of the tube alters the type of movement.

Many of these methods of controlling movement have been discovered by young children – not all of the best ideas come from adults. The adult does however need to be observant in order to support, take advantage of and extend these ideas. Helping the child to note the special features and qualities of the discovery provides encouragement and reinforces their technical understanding and extends designerly thinking, the consideration of a range of possibilities.

'Control' in terms of design and technology is all about a child making things do what they want them to do. This could involve using a programmable toy, but it can also mean making something from scratch with

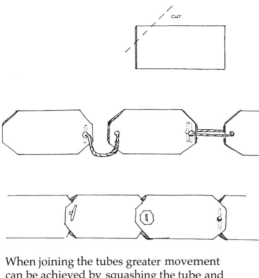

When joining the tubes greater movement
can be achieved by squashing the tube and
cutting off the corners

Children have found that if you change the angle
of the cut you can get a different kind of
movement

The positioning of the tube also affects movement

Figure 6.9 Joining tubes for caterpillars

materials that are readily available in nursery, school or home. Young children are fascinated by things 'that can do something'; this was illustrated in the example of the Holi shooter and in the case of the umbrella project (see Chapter 3) where controlling movement was the result of a good deal of experimentation and modification. Controlling movement does not necessarily involve such complex activity, however. Charlene who made the Holi shooter was able to do this as she had had experiences and activities which scaffolded her development. Being able to put together two pieces of dowel and to use washers to hold cotton reel wheels on a model truck can be just as fulfilling at an early stage. Such small beginnings may fire the imagination and encourage a wide range of adaptations.

The development of hand–eye coordination, spatial awareness and fine

Box 6.6 Controlling movement

Control can be achieved in other ways. When making birds from card tubes Jane found a way of extending the technique to allow for greater movement:

- holes were punched in the tubes;
- an art straw was inserted through the holes;
- wings were attached to the ends of the straw;
- a straw was bent and inserted into the tube and fastened to the straw inside;
- pulling the long straw made the wings flap.

Often children have a vision of what they want to make without having the skills to produce a satisfactory end product. Consequently, when modifications are made the effect is unsatisfactory. This is why adult support is so important. When the child has developed sufficient capability and skill they can achieve a great deal.

Jane was shown how to construct the wings and when she subsequently came to make feet for her bird she had the confidence to discard one idea and try another for herself. Initially they were short straws taped on to the tube but she was unhappy with the effect produced so she punched holes in the bottom of the tube and attached the legs in the same way she had used to make the wings. In effect she had used the technique she had been shown and adapted it to meet her own needs. She was satisfied with the end result.

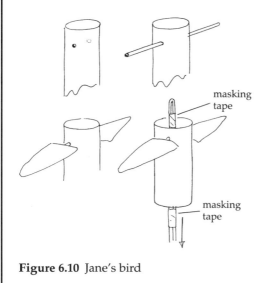

masking tape

masking tape

Figure 6.10 Jane's bird

motor skills are often enhanced through the experience of playing with jigsaws and construction toys. Construction kits are familiar play equipment in most early years settings, yet their full potential is rarely realized. First Gear/Luna Park and other similar kits contain gears as well as structural components. It is a simple matter to temporarily attach items, with Blu-Tack or masking tape, to the cogs to indicate how turning the handle controls direction and speed. While they may be valuable in introducing mechanisms to young children, however, construction kits are particularly useful in developing an early knowledge and understanding of structures. (For information about all of these systems readers should refer to an education supplies catalogue such as Galt or Spectrum.)

Building structures

Construction toys and kits such as Duplo and Lego are 'push–fit' systems where components are readily joined to form structures. There is an apparent progression in such kits; components become smaller as the users become older, however it should not be assumed that manufacturers have all the answers. We have found that young children often prefer using small components rather than large ones. There is also the problem that children are often frustrated by construction kits; there are often insufficient pieces available and, for children in school, there are problems with the generally poor instruction sheets available. The use of focused questioning helps children to highlight why things do connect and do not fall apart. This, as suggested earlier, is 'designerly' questioning; it encourages analytic thinking, a developing understanding of the suitable uses of materials and of how they function. Patterns in construction, qualities that determine strength, rigidity and stability, may all be identified in conversation. For example, children need to learn that stable structures need to be built on a strong and secure base; they should begin to recognize the value of interlacing bricks and the need to provide a framework or shell to mount wheels on a vehicle.

Kits such as Cleversticks, Interstar and Brio may be used to show the advantages of using triangles in construction. A very flexible alternative is provided by the use of art straws, which come in two sizes and are usually supplied with instructional leaflets showing a variety of ways that they can be joined.

Progression can be seen in the complexity of many connecting activities; just as jigsaws become more intricate and complex, so do construction kit products. There are however, a number of ways of extending the uses of apparently simple kits.

The cross-curriculum potential for extended learning is not always explored as construction toys are often used as 'filler activities'. Children can be encouraged to make a model using a kit and provide instructions so that other children can make the same thing. This strategy developed as a result of a group of 5-year-old children evaluating instruction sheets provided with kits, and deciding that they could do better – which they did.

Evaluating products and applications

The development of design and technological literacy may be supported through the evaluation of a whole range of products and environments with which the children are familiar. Toys, food products, sweets and play areas all lend themselves to critical evaluation. We need to consider:

- how far the product/environment meets a clear need;
- its 'fitness for the purpose' intended;
- whether it constitutes an appropriate use of resources;
- what its impact may be beyond the purposes for which it was designed.

(SCAA 1995)

As previously suggested, the priority in the early years is on encouragement and the evaluation of children's own products. It is therefore best conducted by identifying the positive qualities and characteristics that may be used in future work. This is especially important when it comes to the more public final evaluation of designing and making activity. Evaluation sessions developed to round off and share the products of an activity can all too easily degenerate into arguments about whose is 'best'.

As children grow older they will begin to take an interest in a wider and wider range of products and technologies; this should be encouraged. An historical perspective may be introduced to consider the changes in, for example, forms of transportation, heating and lighting. Accounts that emphasize the role of the 'hero inventor' may however, be somewhat misleading (Siraj-Blatchford 1996).

As previously suggested, children should also be encouraged to explore the properties of a range of materials. Textile work provides a particularly useful link between science, design, technology and art. We all wear clothes and are very familiar with their particular qualities. Children soon make it known to adults which clothes they will or will not wear; they may even be encouraged to explain the reasons for their preferences. Clothes are perhaps the most tangible product of textile technology. We can compare costumes and clothing and discuss with the children which ones keep them dry and which keep them warm. We can talk about how they are fastened. What are the different needs that are satisfied by clothing? An extension of this experience could be to examine old, damaged and discarded clothes. These unwanted clothes can be taken apart to help the children see that garments have been constructed from several pieces of fabric; they can look at the seams and the fastenings. An evaluation of the whole garment may include trying it on, judging how it fits and evaluating it for comfort.

Asking questions in science

Early years science and design and technology education should help children to make sense of their world. They will do this through *using* their senses. Well taught science and design and technology therefore emphasizes the use of all the senses: sight, smell, touch and sound can all play a vital role in science and in designing and making. We need to focus the children's attention on detail and also to encourage the children to observe and question. It is through these responses that we can find out more about the children's interests and ideas. They can inform our planning and help us to create an appropriate learning environment.

As research conducted by Bishop and Simpson (1995) has shown, a great deal of learning in nursery science begins with the child exploring materials, artefacts and phenomena through play. The educator then intervenes to enable the learning to develop in particular directions:

> Often the direction of this extension was already decided by the teacher before play had begun. Thus although the nursery teacher would stress the free play situation of the science activity, the materials which had been provided formed a structure and framework for the activity.
>
> (Bishop and Simpson 1995: 6)

A good deal has already been said about the value of intervention through asking questions and about encouraging the children to ask their own questions. This is another area where progression can only be assured by engaging closely with the child. We need to be alert to their interests and mood, be prepared to return to, or build up to, an explanation; as we suggested in Chapter 1, we need to:

- listen to the child – take what they say seriously;
- try to understand what they mean;
- use the child's meaning as the basis for the next adult comment, remark, suggestion, or question;
- try to speak or act in a way that the child understands.

Experimenting and exploring

As previously suggested, a good deal may be achieved by taking an integrated approach to science and design and technology. While designing and making, children can be encouraged to:

- use their senses to explore and recognize the similarities and differences between materials, artefacts and phenomena;
- sort materials into groups on the basis of simple properties, for example, texture, appearance, or transparency. Handling the materials presents the opportunity to learn that materials have different properties, for example, paint or glue soak through some materials and not others;
- recognize that materials have a variety of uses, that materials are chosen for specific uses, which are related to properties.

Progression is achieved by gradually introducing more structure to investigations, and increasingly drawing upon contexts that extend beyond the child's immediate interests and experience. In addition there are two further considerations in planning investigations and explorations:

The introduction and use of scientific instruments and terminology

Instruments that may be used to extend the senses from the earliest years include hand magnifying glasses, binoculars and binocular microscopes and stethoscopes. Measuring equipment such as a simple balance can be used with standard or non-standard units of measurement and decimeter graduated metre sticks are available for use as a preparation for standard distance measurement. Increasingly the use of standard terms and units of measure should be introduced before the children are required to use them in any way themselves. It is our opinion that specialist terminology should be used whenever appropriate; one only needs to consider young children's capacity to recall the names of dinosaurs to realize that we are often overprotective in this respect.

Measurement

Generally speaking, measurement will begin with qualitative terms being applied, like biggest and smallest, furthest and nearest, then middle terms may be added, such as middle-sized, before moving on to non-standard units of measurement and finally to standard measures.

Developing a knowledge and understanding of science

As Vygotsky (1962: 168) observed: 'awareness and deliberate control appear only during a very advanced stage in the development of a mental function, after it has been used and practiced unconsciously and spontaneously'. The approach that we have taken provides a means by which young children may practise science long before they are able to structure their explorations and investigations for themselves or are consciously aware of the cultural value of science and scientific investigation. This applies directly to the processes of science, but it also suggests an approach to the development of a knowledge and understanding of established science. The aim should be to relate this knowledge closely to the child's own experience, responding to the questions and problems they pose themselves in their day-to-day activity and introducing them to experiences that will extend their understandings further. The major emphasis should be on responding to the experiential interests and needs of the children, but a case can be made for prescribing some limited content in preparation for school science (Appendix 4).

To take a concrete example that may be unfamiliar to readers, a good deal could be achieved by introducing more 'air' play to preschools. A whole range of phenomena and scientific understandings are meaningless to young children who have no concept of air as physical matter. Intuition tells us that empty space is just that – empty – that there is nothing in it. But how can we understand gases or the effects of atmospheric pressure as long as we have no concept of air? A great deal can be achieved by introducing young children to experiences that demand the recognition of air as physical matter. We can discuss their understandings as we pour air from one inverted container to another under water. We can run outside with them and hold up cardboard 'sails' that slow us down. We can play with pipes and bubbles and bicycle inner tubes and pumps. We can introduce them to fascinating 'tricks'; if you have never tried holding your finger over a hole in the top of a container full of water and seen how it prevents the water from escaping from another hole at the bottom try it right now – it's well worth it.

This chapter began with a discussion of progression and continuity, we argued that ten distinct 'areas of capability' could be identified and we provided specific guidance on progression within each of them. This provided the third and final element in our general approach to the provision of scaffolding within science and design and technology. The heuristic models provided in Chapter 4 provide another element but it should be emphasized that the references that we have made to discussion and the need to encourage an informed and sustained intellectual engagement with the child is paramount. The more children are encouraged to think about their skills and understandings the more likely it will be that they are empowered to 'transfer' these capabilities, and to apply them in other contexts. Research into this kind of 'metacognition' is still relatively undeveloped but we shall undoubtedly hear more about the subject in the future.

7

Conclusions: the way forward

In Chapter 5 we referred to Edna Mellor's (1953) approach to science and design and technology education. Our central aim in this book has been to provide specialist guidance for early years educators in developing these curriculum areas. This was a task beyond the scope of Mellor's general text but, if we forgive her exclusive use of the masculine personal pronoun, the rationale that she provided all those years ago for developing these subjects at such an early age would be very difficult to improve upon:

> This way of learning through experience is not just 'play', or 'playing about', as it is sometimes called. It is more nearly related to the work of the scientist or craftsman at the bench than to what we adults do when we play in our leisure time. It is the beginning of studies which will one day come to be separated and labeled as physics, geography, chemistry and so on. It is now, when the child's curiosity is intense and his interest widespread that learning takes place at the greatest rate. It is now that sound foundations can be laid for further studies, not only by the acquisition of elementary knowledge, but by the formation of attitudes to work, to discovery and to learning. These attitudes become part of the child's nature and character and will influence his capacity for education at later stages of his growth.

In the foregoing discussions we have identified five key factors in the development of children's science and design and technology capabilities:

- the need to acknowledge the experiences that the child brings from home;
- the stimulation of the child's interest and curiosity;
- the encouragement of both imaginative and purposeful activities;
- seeing things through the child's eyes and supporting their development;
- planning appropriate and relevant 'playful' activities.

The two major theoretical principles upon which these factors are based have been concerned with:

- *Constructivism:* where 'teaching needs to relate to what is familiar to children, not just at the level of the world of events and experiences but also in their world of ideas' (Driver 1985).
- A *'zone of proximal development':* that recognizes that 'awareness and deliberate control appear only during a very advanced stage in the development of a mental function, after it has been used and practised unconsciously and spontaneously' (Vygotsky 1962).

In education it is important that we recognize that tomorrow's adults will have to come to terms with a rate of change that is unprecedented in human history. The curriculum should undoubtedly reflect this. Nothing, however, has been said so far of one form of technology that has been introduced into many preschool and virtually all infant school settings; computers. The price of computer hardware and computer software has come down in recent years although a computer is still likely to represent a major expense for the home or small preschool setting. Given the limited resources available to us we should clearly not be using them simply because 'they are now available' or because we feel that 'computers are important for the future'. We should be more critical. On the face of it, the use of a computer may be considered a fairly limited solitary occupation for the individual child, but the evidence suggests that children tend to use them collaboratively. Computers require turn-taking and other interactive skills but we need to carefully consider what other educational benefits they may bring with them.

Talking encyclopaedias that are accessible to young children are now available on CD-Roms but all computer programmes need to be evaluated carefully before purchase. In fact, to get the most out of the technology it must be recognized that a lot of adult time will need to be invested in the selection of appropriate software and in developing computer related activities that support a rich experiential preschool curriculum rather than detracting the child away from it. In practice this usually requires the use of content-free software such as wordprocessors, drawing and painting programs and databases. However this form of use does open up the possibility of developing an integrated topic approach to computing in the early years. Where there is quality in educational computing it often comes down to this integration; it is not the money spent on the machines or software. Some computer programs have improved beyond the 'drill and practice' and arcade style approaches of the past, but the framework, generic or content-free computer programs still offer much more scope for early years education than the more sophisticated learning packages. It just takes more time to set them up.

As Robert Fulghum (1988) has observed, everything that we really need to know and understand as adults can be learnt in the preschool. We have been concerned to provide the kind of guidance in these pages that will support just this kind of 'transferable' learning. The following, adapted from Fulghum (1988), lists what it was that he felt he had learnt in his preschool, and, with a little extrapolation into the terms of the grown-up world, it is clearly possible to apply them to our interactions with family and in our working lives, if not in the operation of our governments and international relations.

The most important things to be learnt in the pre-school:
Share everything.
Play fair.
Don't hit people.
Put things back where you found them.
Clean up your own mess.
Don't take things that aren't yours.
Say you're sorry when you hurt somebody.
Wash your hands before you eat.
Flush the toilet after you use it.
Fruit and vegetables are good for you.
Live a balanced life – learn a bit, think a bit, and draw and paint and sing and dance and play and work a bit every day.
Take a nap every afternoon.
When you are out in the world watch out for the traffic, and stick together.
Be aware of wonder (remember the little seed you saw in the Styrofoam cup: the roots went down and the plant went up and nobody really knows how or why, but we are all just like that).
Goldfish and hamsters and white mice and even the little seed in the Styrofoam cup – they all die. So do we.
The first word we all learn – the biggest word of all – LOOK.

As Fulghum suggests; 'everything we need to know is in there somewhere'. All of these things can be learnt in the early years – they should be

– and they shouldn't be forgotten. Their understanding requires a knowledge of a wide range of subjects in addition to science, design and technology, and they also require the development of important skills and attitudes as well. As Fulghum says, we need to keep our sense of wonder, we must keep on looking and 'Think what a better world it would be if we all . . . the whole world . . . had cookies and milk about three o'clock every afternoon and then lay down with our blankets for a nap' (1988: 7). We feel that constitutes good advice for all of us.

● ● ● Appendix 1

Towards a compendium of scientific explanations

While we would have liked to have provided an extended compendium of answers to some of the most common questions that children ask, this was beyond the scope of this publication. The following are offered as an example of the sorts of questions children ask and as examples of the kind of answers that we feel most appropriate. Appendix 2 provides lists of resources that might be used to find the answers to many other questions. In providing these answers we fully recognize that very young children are unlikely to understand everything at once. We don't feel that should influence us unduly, however. We have found that it is often easier to provide a full explanation than to assess which part they are ready for. The intention is not, at this stage, to formally 'teach' the child the scientific principles. Children will often let you know at what point their curiosity has been satisfied and when it is time to drop the subject. The thing to remember is that by providing an explanation you are doing two things that are vital if the child is to grow up with a respect and appreciation for science:

1 You will have legitimized the question that they have asked and rewarded their curiosity.
2 You will also have shown that science is able to provide the answers to many of our questions. (Note: In helping the child to develop an early recognition of the kinds of questions that are open to scientific explanation and those that are not, you will also be making an important contribution to their spiritual education.)

Our intention in providing these answers is therefore far from prescriptive, the answers are not definitive, and they should be adapted in practice to fit the particular child, their age, their previous knowledge and the specific context in which the question is asked.

Why is the sky blue?

Let's start by thinking about the Earth and the sky to begin with. This is the planet Earth that we live on . . . Is this how you imagine it? Is this the shape that you have seen in pictures?

The chances are that a child will say that they have seen pictures (even if they have been on cartoon programmes) that show it as 'round'. This might be a good time to take out a globe, but you should say, 'That's right, I'm sorry I just drew the rock part – now I need to draw the stuff that fills in all these cracks and hollow bits and makes the Earth look so smooth and round from space'.

It's now time to draw a blue circle that encloses the 'rock' and to colour it blue. We can then ask what the blue stuff is called and can agree that that is the ocean and that it is held on to the Earth by 'gravity' – which is a force that holds everything down towards the centre of the planet.

Then we can draw another circle outside of that and tell the child that the Earth has another ocean that we live in and that is the ocean of air that we breathe; it is held on in the same way as the ocean of water – by gravity, so it doesn't drift off into space. We call it the 'atmosphere'.

You now have the basic building blocks of an answer; the idea that we live in an ocean of air and that that is what we look up at and call the sky. At night the sky looks black, and that is also the way the 'sky' looks from space. What we are actually seeing during the day is a reflection of sunlight on a mixture of gases, dust and water vapour (like steam) high up in the atmosphere. The reflection is blue because the light is being scattered by these tiny pieces of dust and water vapour. It's the same reason that cigarette smoke is blue; you can also demonstrate the effect by putting a drop or two of milk in a glass of water and holding it up to a light. You will find it takes on a blue tint.

Why is the sea blue?

The sea looks blue because it reflects the light coming from the blue sky.

What is frost and how does it get on the windows?

There is always moisture (water vapour) in the air and when the air temperature drops below the freezing point of water (0° on the centigrade scale) this moisture is left as ice crystals on the ground or any other exposed object that is just as cold. If a building is left with no heating on then it will be left on the windows.

Why is the grass all wet in the morning?

When the air has a lot of moisture in it and the temperature of the ground is lower than the air, the water in contact with it changes from vapour back to its liquid form as water (it condenses) and the droplets are formed.

Why do things float?

Like many scientific questions this one sounds deceptively simple. To answer it fully requires the measurement of both the object and the proposed fluid's weight and volume. It is only when we consider the relative density of the two that we can determine if floatation will occur. These are ideas that the child will be introduced to later in their education, so for the meantime we should answer that it is because 'the water is pushing it up'. This concept of 'upthrust' will be very useful to them in progressively developing their understanding of the overall process. Upthrust can be demonstrated quite easily, simply invite the child to push something under the water and ask them what it is that they feel as they do so. Have them compare the upthrust of objects that are very buoyant (e.g. Polystyrene) with objects that are less so (e.g. wood). If you do this in a bowl or a standard waterplay tank you could also usefully draw their attention to the fact that the water level rises as they push things under the surface (it is the weight of this displaced water that provides the upthrust).

What are bubbles?

Drinks 'fizz' when the gas (carbon dioxide) that has been dissolved in the liquid during manufacture is released. The can or bottle is closed under pressure but as soon as the container is opened the gas is able to come out. The gas bubbles are lighter than water so they float to the surface. To help children understand why it is that the bubbles are spherical you might begin by asking them to make themselves as small as they possibly can. That is what the gas has to do when it is released in the liquid that is squashing it from all sides. It makes the smallest shape it can and this is 'round'. When we blow into a tube held under water we make our own bubbles in the same way and soap bubbles are formed in a similar way. When we blow a bubble there is air trapped inside the soap film and it is squashed into the smallest space available by this 'elastic' film.

What will the moon look like tomorrow?

The moon is constantly moving in a big circle around the Earth. We can see it because of the sunlight shining on it. We only see it when it is on our side of the Earth and we can see it best during the night because it looks so bright against the black sky all around it. The moon looks a different shape sometimes because the sun is only lighting up one side of it leaving the other side in shadow.

As the moon moves around the Earth the sunlight increasingly falls on the other side so we see less and less of it until the whole side of the moon facing the Earth is in shadow. This is what we call a new moon. A full moon is seen when all of the side of the moon that is facing us is lit up.

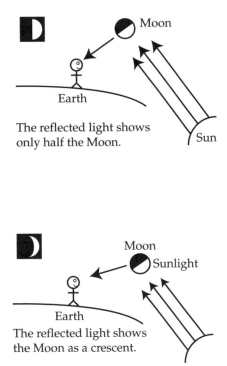

The reflected light shows only half the Moon.

The reflected light shows the Moon as a crescent.

What happens when you mix vinegar and baking soda?

Baking soda and baking powder are used in baking to produce millions of little bubbles in the dough or batter mixture, which makes it rise up and make a light, spongy cake rather than something as flat as a pancake. The active ingredients in baking soda and baking powder is a harmless chemical called sodium bicarbonate. 'Carbonates' turn into gas (carbon dioxide) whenever they are heated (for example in making a cake) or when they are mixed with an acid. Vinegar is an acid (a solution of acetic acid).

What happened to the tadpoles?

They grow legs and become frogs. We call this process 'metamorphosis'. Some other amphibians and some fish do the same thing; at a certain stage in their life they change their body to suit a new diet and a new way of living. (Insects metamorphose also, for example, caterpillars turn into butterflies following their metamorphosis in a pupa.)

How does the electric torch work?

The battery inside the torch is full of chemicals that store electrical energy. When it is connected to a bulb all of the energy is forced through the very thin wire that you can see inside the glass (use a magnifying lens if you have one). If the battery is running out of energy you can see that it still makes the wire red hot. When the battery is new the wire gets so hot it is white hot and that is where the light comes from. The glass stops the wire burning in the air and protects us from being burnt too, but the glass does get warm. You shouldn't touch big lamp bulbs at home when they are on because they get very hot.

What happens to the water when it goes down to the sea?

To understand what happens we need to think a bit about how puddles dry up and about the steam that comes out of a boiling kettle. When a kettle boils we can see some of the water changing from a liquid into a vapour but this even happens when water isn't boiling. We call this 'evaporation'; it's just as well it happens or the washing would never dry when we leave it on the line outside. The water in a puddle gradually evaporates as the water becomes a vapour in the air. This is the way that clouds are formed. After the water goes down to the sea some of it evaporates and forms clouds, which later 'break' to cause rain to fall. The rain runs down through the drains and rivers to the sea and the cycle repeats itself over and over again, watering plants and providing water for our reservoirs in the process.

Why do your feet feel cold when you stand on a tiled floor with no shoes on?

While the idea that the 'cold' from the floor is coming into your feet may seem attractive, that isn't what is happening at all. It's actually the sensation of the heat leaving your feet that you can feel. A carpet wouldn't let the heat flow away from you so easily, it would provide 'insulation'. The tiles are good heat 'conductors', however, so you lose the heat and feel 'cold'.

Do light things fall more slowly than heavy things?

No, they don't usually, but they might if they have more air resistance (that's due to 'friction'). Try running down the playground with, and without, a big square or rectangular board held out in front of you. The air really slows you down if you get in its way. It is usually this air resistance that makes things fall more slowly. Think of a parachute and imagine how quickly someone would fall if they jumped out of an aeroplane without one. Designers are concerned to develop modern cars that 'cut' through the air easily and save petrol, so they streamline them.

● ● ● Appendix 2

Where to go for further information

Books

Asimov, A. (1987) *Asimov's New Guide to Science: A Revised Edition*. London: Penguin Books.

Bronowski, J. (1979) *The Ascent of Man*. London: British Broadcasting Corporation (BBC).

Bunch, B. and Hellemans, A. (1993) *The Timetables of Technology*. New York: Simon & Schuster.

Farrow, S. (1996) *The Really Useful Science Book*. London: Falmer Press.

Feasey, R. (1993) Scientific investigations, in R. Sherrington (ed.) *The ASE Primary Science Teachers' Handbook*. Cheltenham: Stanley Thornes.

Goldsworthy, A. and Feasey, R. (1994) *Making Sense of Primary Science Investigations*. Hatfield: Association of Science Education (ASE).

Lafferty, P. and Rowe, J. (eds) (1993) *The Hutchinson Dictionary of Science*. Oxford: Helicon.

Pacey, A. (1994) *The Culture of Technology*. Cambridge, MA: MIT Press.

Sherrington, R. (ed.) (1993) *The ASE Primary Science Teachers' Handbook*. Cheltenham: Stanley Thornes.

Siraj-Blatchford, J. and Siraj-Blatchford, I. (eds) (1995) *Educating the Whole Child: Cross-Curricular Skills, Themes and Dimensions*. Buckingham: Open University Press.

Siraj-Blatchford, J. (1996) *Learning Science, Technology and Social Justice*. Nottingham: Education Now.

Wensham, M. (1995) *Understanding Primary Science: Ideas, Concepts and Explanations*. London: Paul Chapman.

Places to visit

Eureka! The Museum for Children, Halifax – hands-on communications, inventions etc. Tel: 01422 330069.

Exploratory Hands-on Science Centre, Bristol – Hands-on science and technology. Tel: 01179 079000.

Greens Mill, Sneinton, Nottingham – Hands-on science, working windmill. Tel: 0115 9156878.

Legoland, Windsor – Lego theme park. Tel: 0990 626364.

Museum of Science and Industry, Manchester – Transport and hands-on science centre. Tel: 0161 8322244.

North of England Open-Air Museum, Beamish – Re-creation of life in the early twentieth century. Tel: 01207 231811.

Satrosphere, Aberdeen – Hands-on science and technology. Tel: 01224 213232.

Science Museum, London – Interactive display galleries. Tel: 0171 938 8000

Snibston Discovery Park, Coalville, Leics. – Science and industry, interactive displays. Tel: 01530 510851.

Techniquest, Cardiff – Hands-on science and technology centre. Tel: 01222 481919.

Transperience, Bradford – Interactive transport museum. Tel: 01274 690909.

Appendix 3

An outline scheme for addressing the misconceptions of 'race' in the early years

Children of 3 to 6 years of age commonly exhibit curiosity about physical differences and they often show racialized preferences. At this age the children develop their identity as family members and they can also absorb their family's stereotypes and racial biases. It is at this stage that they begin to classify people into groups and to develop theories about why people are different. It is also at this stage, when they are forming their first friendships, that we can do the most to support them in learning to accept diversity and feel comfortable with differences. As previously suggested, scientists used to think that human beings could be split up into different groups or 'races', but the study of genetics has now shown that the differences between people in any one population are enormous in comparison to any differences that can be found between populations. We can therefore now say with confidence that 'race' has no biological significance for human beings. The differences that we see between groups really are only 'skin deep'.

The following scheme may be pursued with a group of children acting as a 'collective scientist' – with the educator directing the discussion and structuring the activity in the manner suggested in Chapter 4. It will provide some preparation for work to be carried out in school at Key Stage One of the National Curriculum on variation and classification where they will be taught:

(a) to recognise similarities and differences between themselves and other pupils;

(b) that living things can be grouped according to observable similarities and differences.

(DfE 1995b: 4)

Parents may usefully participate in the activities and might prepare for the activity by discussing what it is that the National Curriculum is referring to and by making a list of all the groups of which they and their child are members. They could then share this list in a brainstorm session. The product of this brainstorm, which is likely to include family, gender and religious groups, could be extended to include more subtle groupings such as, hair, eye colour, complexion and skin colour.

They might then join the children and be included in the initial brainstorm of 'In what ways are we all the same?' The discussion is likely to begin with references to physiology (one head, two arms) and this should be encouraged before going onto more subtle similarities like 'we all eat food' and cultural similarities such as 'we all speak English in school'. The aim is to produce the biggest possible list of similarities. This should be displayed prominently and referred to frequently throughout the programme.

The next stage is to carry out a series of investigations with the group that explore a number of ways in which the children differ from each other. The following are provided as suggestions and the investigations should be continued until the children clearly accept that 'every single one of them is different' (the investigations all show continuous variations).

'Simon says' the oldest children in the class are the biggest. Is this true? The children can draw silhouettes of each other (standing against paper pinned to the wall). You put the age in months on each and display them on the wall in order. Then ask, 'Are the oldest the tallest?' 'What have we learnt?' The conclusions will probably be, 'We are all different heights' and 'We are (nearly?) all different ages' should again be displayed along with the findings from each of the following:

'Simon says' that people with longer legs can jump further. Is that true? (see the Introduction).

'Simon says' there are only three skin colours. Is that true? Each child draws their face and is supported in mixing paint to match as closely as they can their own skin colour. The pictures are then sorted and discussed.

'Simon says' if you are bigger you are stronger. Is that true? The silhouettes can be used again for this. A 'measure' of strength can be obtained by pushing on some bathroom scales.

'Simon says' the bigger your hand is the more marbles you can pick up. Is that true? The hands can be silhouetted and the number of marbles drawn onto them.

The children can then put together all of their findings and compare themselves with the others, e.g. the head and the hand can be attached to the silhouette in a display.

If the programme is to be combined with INSET or an out of school/centre parent workshop this would be a good time to discuss:

- the implications of increased mixed parentage;
- the Children Act and the UN Convention on the Rights of the Child;
- the historical and contemporary relationship between so called 'race' groups;
- the importance of positive role models.

A crucial concept relates to our tendency to essentialize the differences we see in 'others' while we take the similarities between ourselves for granted.

As a final activity the children could identify the groups that they belong to in terms of gender, home language, favourite hobbies, favourite colours, favourite pets, favourite food, eye colours etc. Venn diagrams can be used to produce displays that show that the groups are usually mutually exclusive, and that the groups that are important to them cut across gender, ethnicity etc. In a multiethnic group of children and parents, two inherited characteristics that are not related to ethnicity might also be included: tongue curling and ear lobes. It's just a fact of nature that we are not all able to curl our tongue in our mouths and we don't all have droopy ear lobes. If you don't believe it take a look. There is no significance whatsoever to these variations. They are inherited characteristics of no importance at all – just like skin colour.

● ● ● Appendix 4

Working towards the National Curriculum for science

Life processes and physical things

At Key Stage 1 work on the life processes should be related to the children's knowledge of animals and plants in their local environment. A good deal of this knowledge can be developed before they go to school. In Appendix 3 we have provided details of work that could contribute significantly to the children's knowledge and understanding of humans as organisms, of variation and classification. Preschool education can also contribute by developing the child's recognition of a wide range of plants and animals. In doing so it should be recognized that there can be no adequate substitute for physical contact with live specimens. Handling these with care and respect is vital, and safety should also be considered, for example, a lot of common plants and shrubs are poisonous (see Appendix 6).

Materials and their properties

The National Curriculum at Key Stage 1 suggests that children should learn about the names, uses and properties of everyday materials. They should also learn that the shape and form of materials can be changed. The use of a wide range of materials in preschool design and technology work will contribute a great deal to all of this.

Physical processes

The emphasis at Key Stage 1 is on the observable effects of electricity, forces and motion, light and sound. Again there are numerous opportunities to introduce and discuss these effects in a preschool context. Where concepts are especially challenging, as in the case of forces, an early introduction may be especially valuable. As we have already suggested, time might usefully be provided to introduce some 'air play' into preschool settings. This would provide a valuable grounding for ideas about air resistance and friction.

Remember, the outdoor environment provides a major resource for the development of knowledge and understanding in science so it is worth getting to know the resources that you have at your disposal really well. While the business of mastering all the relevant animal and plant taxonomies may seem daunting, much less time and effort is needed to learn the names of those varieties in the immediate vicinity of the preschool setting. In fact the task of finding out about the environment could initially be shared out among the setting staff. Even with this limited knowledge you will be able to provide the children with an extremely valuable introduction to science, and as previously suggested you will also be teaching them some important attitudes; you will be showing that you value scientific knowledge and that a body of knowledge is available to satisfy their curiosity when they have a question.

• • • Appendix 5

Material resources

References have been made to Technology Teaching Systems (TTS) in the book and their *Technology and Science* catalogue may provide a useful starting point in deciding what you need. It is available from: TTS, Monk Road, Alfreton, DE55 7RL Tel. 01773 830255 Fax: 01773 830325. As Glauert (1998) has suggested, many of the resources that are needed for science are everyday, non-specialist materials; the real challenge is in collecting and organizing them. Safety is crucial in this aspect and every centre/setting should have a copy of the Association for Science Education (1990) booklet called *Be Safe,* and the National Association of Advisors and Inspectors in Design and Technology (NAAIDT 1992) notes, *Make it Safe;* between the two they outline all of the major issues (see Appendix 6).

The following starter list of resources has been adapted from a list provided by Glauert (1998):

- *exploring materials:* water, sand, soil, sawdust, clay, Plasticine, paint, salt, flour, oil, vinegar, liquid soap, glycerine, cooking ingredients, flavourings and colourings;
- *construction materials:* a variety of construction kits, bricks and blocks of different shapes and sizes;
- *recycled materials:* containers of different materials and sizes, for example, cardboard boxes, plastic pots, a variety of papers and fabrics;
- *living things:* plants, seeds, bulbs, and minibeasts, for example, aquarium, snails, caterpillars;
- *collections:* metal, wood, plastic, fabrics, threads and strings etc. *Objects*

with different properties, for example, transparent/translucent/opaque; rough/smooth; stretchy or bendy; magnetic; floating/sinking. *Collections of natural materials*, for example, fruits and seeds, shells, stones, feathers;

- *equipment for measurement and observation:* magnifying glasses, measuring equipment, for example, scales, spring balances, rules, stopwatches, egg timers, thermometers, measuring jugs;
- *work bench(es):* tools, sandpaper, wood off-cuts, cotton reels, nails, fastenings, objects to explore and take apart, such as telephones, clocks, cassette recorders, radios.

● ● ● Appendix 6

Safety and hygiene

Reference has already been made to essential publications:

Association for Science Education (ASE) (1990) *Be Safe!* Available from the ASE at College Lane, Hatfield, Herts. AL10 9AA Tel. 01707 267411.
National Association of Advisors and Inspectors in Design and Technology (NAAIDT 1992) *Make it Safe.* Available from TTS (see Appendix 5).

Preliminary guidance

Design and technology is a practical subject area where children are encouraged to be independent makers, to develop skills in using tools and materials. A number of different approaches and attitudes to working with tools can currently be found in early years settings. Some settings restrict the children's access to tools in the belief that this is safe working practice; others seem unaware of the potential dangers or introduce dangerous and inappropriate working practices. We need to provide opportunities for children to work with a range of suitable tools but at the same time we should teach and enforce some simple safety rules to help to keep them safe.

Misuse of scissors is perhaps the most common cause of injury. Keep scissors free from glue, as accidents often happen when children are struggling with inadequate tools. In fact many of the potential dangers can be avoided if tools are used for their intended purpose. A common mistake is to use scissors to make a hole, when hole punches and tapered reamers are much more suitable tools. Making a hole in a box or plastic bottle should not be done with a pair of scissors; they can easily slip. The safest tool with which to make holes is a tapered reamer.

- treat tools and materials with respect;
  - they will last longer;
  - they are less likely to cause injury if they are looked after and used correctly;
- model good practice;
  - if children are to be prepared adequately they must be shown safe and appropriate ways of handling tools. Whenever we use tools, we should always select the correct tool for the job;
- use appropriate materials;
  - remember that common plants and shrubs may be poisonous (see *Be Safe* above for a detailed list);
- use space wisely – avoid distractions.

Food safety

Children need to know about safe and hygienic ways to work with food. Because it is such a familiar activity there is a tendency to treat procedures for food preparation with less respect than we should. We must be wary of becoming complacent in the ways that food is handled. Preparation points to remember:

- wash implements before use;
- clean work surfaces with Dettox or Milton;
- a wipe-clean covering may be used on tables but remember that this should only be used for food technology;
- wear an apron;
- wash hands;
- check the children's medical records for possible allergies;
- avoid using nuts;
- buy food as it is needed and avoid storing items unnecessarily;
- check the shelf-life of consumables and strictly adhere to this advice;
- keep items such as flour in airtight containers;
- store utensils in covered containers and wash before and after use.

References

Abbott, L., Marsh, C., Griffin, B. *et al.* (1996) *Firm Foundations: Quality Education in the Early Years,* A Video Resource Pack. Manchester: Manchester Metropolitan University.

Asimov, A. (1987) *Asimov's New Guide to Science: A Revised Edition.* London: Penguin Books.

Assessment and Performance Unit (APU) (1987) *Design and Technological Activity: A Framework for Assessment.* London: DES, HMSO.

Assessment and Performance Unit (APU) (1991) *The Assessment of Performance in Design and Technology: Final Report.* London: School Examination and Assessment Authority, HMSO.

Association for Science Education (ASE) (1990) *Be Safe! Some Aspects of Safety in School Science and Technology for Key Stage 1 and 2.* Hatfield: ASE.

Association for Science Education (ASE) (1998) *Report of the Science Education 2000+ Task Group.* Hatfield: ASE.

Bandura, A. (1986) *The Social Foundation of Thought and Action: A Social Cognitive Theory.* Englewood Cliffs, NJ: Prentice Hall.

Bentley, D. and Watts, M. (1994) *Primary Science and Technology.* Buckingham: Open University Press.

Bishop, A. and Simpson, R. (1995) Strategies for structured play in science in the nursery. *Primary Teaching Studies,* 9(3): 5–9.

Black, P. (1993) The Purposes of Science Education, in R. Sherrington (ed.) *ASE Primary Science Teachers' Handbook.* Cheltenham: Stanley Thornes.

Braben, D. (1994) *To be a Scientist.* Oxford: Oxford University Press.

Bronowski, J. (1979) *The Ascent of Man.* London: British Broadcasting Corporation (BBC).

Brooks, A. and Driver, R. (1989) *The Development of Pupils' Understanding of the*

Physical Characteristics of Air. Leeds: University of Leeds, Centre for Studies in Science and Mathematics Education.

Brown, C. (1993) Bridging the gender gap in science and technology: how long will it take? *International Journal of Technology and Design Education*, 3(2): 65–73.

Brown, G. and Wragg, E. (1993) *Questioning*. London: Routledge.

Bruce, T. (1991) *Time to Play in Early Childhood Education*. London: Hodder and Stoughton.

Bruner, J. (1966) *Towards a Theory of Instruction*. Cambridge, MA: Harvard University Press.

Bunch, B. and Hellemans, A. (1993) *The Timetables of Technology*. New York: Simon & Schuster.

Christofides-Henriques, A. (1984) 'On the experimental behaviour of primary school children', mimeo. University of Geneva.

Craft, A. (1997) *Can You Teach Creativity?* Nottingham: Education Now.

Curie, E. (1942) *Madame Curie* (translated by V. Sheean). London: The Reprint Society.

Dansky, J. and Silverman, I. (1973) Effects of play on associative fluency in preschool aged children. *Developmental Psychology*, 9: 38–43.

Davenport, G. (1994) *An Introduction to Child Development*. London: Collins Educational.

Day, M. (1988) Primary science: the hidden challenge in M. Clarkson (ed.) *Emerging Issues in Primary Education*. London: Falmer Press.

de Bono, E. (1977) *De Bono's Thinking Course*. London: British Broadcasting Company.

Department of Education and Science (DES) (1985) *Education for All, The Swann Report*. London: HMSO.

Department for Education (DfE) (1995a) *Design and Technology in the National Curriculum*. London: DfE, HMSO.

Department for Education (DfE) (1995b) *Science in the National Curriculum*. London: DfE, HMSO.

DeVries, R. (1997) Piaget's social theory. *Educational Researcher*, 26(2) March: 5–17.

Donaldson, M. (1978) *Children's Minds*. London: Fontana.

Donaldson, M. (1992) *Human Minds: An Exploration*. London: Penguin Press.

Driver, R. (1985) *The Pupil as Scientist*. Milton Keynes: Open University Press.

Driver, R., Leach, J., Millar, R. and Scott, P. (1996) *Young People's Images of Science*. Buckingham: Open University Press.

Farrow, S. (1996) *The Really Useful Science Book*. London: Falmer Press.

Feasey, R. (1993) Scientific investigations, in R. Sherrington, (ed.) *The ASE Primary Science Teachers' Handbook*. Cheltenham: Stanley Thornes.

Feasey, R. and Siraj-Blatchford, J. (1998) *Key Skills in Science: Communication*. Durham: Tyneside TEC/University of Durham.

Fleer, M. (ed.) (1996) *Play Through the Profiles: Profiles Through Play*. Watson, ACT: Australian Early Childhood Association.

Fleer, M. and Hardy, T. (1996) *Science for Children: Developing a Personal Approach to Teaching*, Sydney: Prentice Hall.

Ford, J. (1975) *Paradigms and Fairy Tales: An Introduction to the Science of Meanings*, Vol. 1. London: Routledge and Kegan Paul.

Foulds, K., Gott, R. and Feasey, R. (1992) *Investigative Work in Science*, report of the Exploration of Science Project, commissioned by the National Curriculum Council, Durham.

Frobel, F. (1987) *The Education of Man* (Trans. W. Hailman) New York: Appleton & Co.

Fulghum, R. (1988) *All I Really Need to Know I Learned in Kindergarten*. New York: Villard Books.

Gardner, H. (1991) *The Unschooled Mind: How Children Think and How Schools Teach*. London: Fontana.

Gardner, P. (1995) The relationship between technology and science: some historical and philosophical reflections: part II. *International Journal of Science Education*, 14(5): 563–78.

Glauert, E. (1998) Science in the early years, in I. Siraj-Blatchford (ed.) *A Curriculum Development Handbook for Early Childhood Educators*. Stoke-on-Trent: Trentham Books.

Gott, R., Feasey, R. and Foulds, K. (1991) *Science Explorations*. London: National Curriculum Council (now SCAA Publications).

Hall, S. (1992) Race, culture and communications: looking backward and forward in cultural studies. *Rethinking Marxism*, 5: 10–18.

Harding, S. (1991) *Whose Science? Whose Knowledge? Thinking from Women's Lives*. Buckingham: Open University Press.

Harding, S. (ed.) (1993) *The 'Racial' Economy of Science*. Bloomington, IN: Indiana University Press.

Harlen, W. (1992) *Teaching and Learning Primary Science*. London: Paul Chapman.

Hodson, D. (1990) A critical look at practical work in school science. *School Science Review*, 70(256): 33–40.

Hohmann, M., Banet, B. and Weikart, D. (1979) *Young Children in Action: A Manual for Preschool Educators*. Ypsilanti, MI: High/Scope Press.

Holt, J. (1991) *Learning All the Time*. Nottingham: Education Now.

Hurst, V. and Joseph, J. (1998) *Supporting Early Learning: The Way Forward*. Buckingham: Open University Press.

Ihde, D. (1983) The historical–ontological priority of technology over science, in P. Durbin and F. Rapp (eds) *Philosophy and Technology*, Boston Studies in the Philosophy of Science, 80. Dordrecht: D. Reidel.

Johnson, S. and Murphy, P. (1986) *Girls and Physics, Reflections on Assessment and Performance Unit Findings*, APU Occasional Paper No. 4. London: DES and APU.

Johnston, J. (1996) *Early Explorations in Science*. Buckingham: Open University Press.

Kenway, J. Blackmore, J., Willis, S. and Rennie, L. (1996) The emotional dimensions of feminist pedagogy in schools, in P. Murphy and C. Gipps (eds) (1996) *Equity in the Classroom: Towards Effective Pedagogy for Girls and Boys*. London: UNESCO Publishing and Falmer Press.

Laevers, F. (1993) *An Exploration of the Concept of Involvement as an Indicator for Quality in Early Childhood Care and Education*. Dundee: Scottish Consultative Council on the Curriculum.

Layton, D. (1993) *Technology's Challenge to Science Education*. Buckingham: Open University Press.

Layton, D., Jenkins, E., MacGill, S. and Davey, A. (1993) *Inarticulate Science? Perspectives on the Public Understanding of Science and Some Implications for Science Education*. Nafferton: Studies in Education.

Levi-Strauss, C. (1994) *Structural Anthropology: 2*. London: Penguin Books.

MacNaughton, G. (1995) A poststructural approach to learning in early childhood settings, in M. Fleer (ed.) *DAPcentrism: Challenging Developmentally Appropriate Practice*. Watson, ACT: Australian Early Childhood Association, (pp. 35–54).

Mellor, E. (1953) *Education Through Experience in the Infant School Years*. Oxford: Basil Blackwell.

Millar, R. (1989) What is 'scientific method' and can it be taught? in J. Wellington (ed.) *Skills and Processes in Science Education*. London: Routledge.

Millar, R. and Driver, R. (1987) Beyond processes. *Studies in Science Education*, 14: 33–62.

Montessori, M. (1912) *Montessori Method* (translated by A. George). London: Heinemann.

Murphy, P. and Gipps, C. (1996) *Equity in the Classroom: Towards Effective Pedagogy for Girls and Boys*. London: Falmer, UNESCO.

National Association of Advisors and Inspectors in Design and Technology (NAAIDT) (1992) *Make it Safe*. Eastleigh: NAAIDT.

Newton, D. (1992) Observation, investigation and the National Curriculum for England and Wales. *Evaluation and Research in Education*, 6(2, 3): 94–106.

Nuffield Design and Technology Project (1995) *Key Stage Three Materials and Teachers Guide*. London: Longman.

Nutbrown, C. (ed.)(1996) *Respectful Educators: Capable Learners*. London: Paul Chapman.

Pacey, A. (1994) *The Culture of Technology*. Cambridge, MA: MIT Press.

Peat, F. (1996) *Blackfoot Physics: A Journey into the Native American Universe*. London: Fourth Estate.

Penfold, J. (1988) *Craft, Design and Technology: Past, Present and Future*. Stoke-on-Trent: Trentham Books.

Pepler, D. (1982) Play and divergent thinking, in D. Peplar and K. Rubin (eds) *The Play of Children: Current Research and Theory*. Basel: Kargen.

Piaget, J. (1962) *Play, Dreams and Imitation in Childhood*. London: Routledge and Kegan Paul.

Polanyi, N. (1973) *Personal Knowledge: Towards a Post Critical Philosophy*. London: Routledge and Kegan Paul.

Rosenberg, N. (1982) *Inside the Black Box: Technology and Economics*. Cambridge: Cambridge University Press.

Rubin, K., Fein, G. and Vandenberg, B. (1983) Play, in E. Hetherington and P. Mussen (eds) *Handbook of Child Psychology, Vol. 4: Socialization, Personality and Social Development*. New York: Wiley.

School Curriculum and Assessment Authority (SCAA) (1995) *Design and Technology in the National Curriculum*. London: HMSO.

School Curriculum and Assessment Authority (SCAA) (1996) *Desirable Outcomes for Children's Learning*. London: DfEE/SCAA, DfEE.

Schools Council (1975) *Ethics and Education Project: Environment*. London: Longman.

Schweinhart, L., Barnes, H. and Weikart, D. (1993) *Significant Benefits: The High/Scope Perry Preschool Study Through Age 27*. Ypsilanti, MI: The High/Scope Press.

Scott, C. (1996) Science for the west, myth for the rest?, in L. Nader (ed.) *Naked Science: Anthropological Inquiry into Boundaries, Power, and Knowledge*. London: Routledge.

Scottish Development Education Centre (SDEC) (1994) *Technology: Who Needs It? A Global Approach to Technology*. Edinburgh: SDEC.

Sherrington, R. (ed.) (1993) *The ASE Primary Science Teachers' Handbook*. Cheltenham: Stanley Thornes.

Siraj-Blatchford, J. and Siraj-Blatchford, I. (eds) (1995) *Educating the Whole Child: Cross-curricular Skills, Themes and Dimensions*. Buckingham: Open University Press.

Siraj-Blatchford, J. (1996) *Learning Science, Technology and Social Justice*. Nottingham: Education Now.

Siraj-Blatchford, I. (ed.) (1998) *A Curriculum Development Handbook for Early Childhood Educators*. Stoke-on-Trent: Trentham Books.

Siraj-Blatchford, J. and Coates, D. (1995) Design and technology, in K. Ashcroft and D. Palacio (eds) *A Primary Teacher's Guide to the New National Curriculum*. London: Falmer Press.

Siraj-Blatchford, J. and Patel, L. (1995) Understanding education for the primary classroom, in J. Siraj-Blatchford and I. Siraj-Blatchford (eds) *Educating the Whole Child: Cross-curricular Skills, Themes and Dimensions*. Buckingham: Open University Press.

Siraj-Blatchford, I. and Clarke, P. (in press) *Supporting Early Learning: Identity, Diversity and Language*. Buckingham: Open University Press.

Smith, P. (1994) Play and the uses of play, in J. Moyles (ed.) *The Excellence of Play*. Buckingham: Open University Press.

Steiner, R. (1968) *Practical Courses for Teachers*. Bristol: Rudolph Steiner Press.

Stenhouse, L. (1978) *An Introduction to Curriculum Research and Development*. London: Heinemann.

Stewart, D. (1990) *The Right to Movement: Motor Development in Every School*. London: Falmer Press.

Sylva, K. (1992) Conversations in the nursery: how they contribute to aspirations and plans. *Language and education*, 6(2, 3 & 4): 147–8.

Sylva, K., Bruner, J. and Genova, P. (1979) The role of play in the problem-solving of children 3–5 years old, in J. Bruner, A. Jolly and K. Sylva (eds) *Play, Its Role and Development*. Harmondsworth: Penguin.

Sylva, K., Meluish, E., Sammonds, P. and Siraj-Blatchford, I. (1996) *Effective Provision of Preschool Education: A Proposal to the DfEE*. London: University of London, Institute of Education.

Thorpe, S., Deshpande, P. and Edwards, C. (eds) (1994) *Race, Equality and Science Teaching: A Teachers Handbook*. Hatfield: ASE.

Tizard, B. and Hughes, M. (1984) *Young Children Learning*. London: Fontana.

Vines, G. (1996) New! Improved Formula. *Times Higher Educational Supplement* (THES), Opinion, October 11: 19.

Vygotsky, L. (1962) *Thought and Language*. Cambridge, MA: MIT Press.

Vygotsky, L. (1978) *Mind in Society: The Development of Higher Psychological Processes*, Cambridge MA: Harvard University Press.

Webster, L. (1997) Science assignment, extract reproduced with permission. Unpublished BSc (Ed.) University of Durham School of Education.

Weikart, D., Rogers, L., Adcock, C. and McClelland, D. (1971) *The Cognitively Orientated Curriculum: A Framework for Preschool Teachers*. Urbana, IL: University of Illinois.

Wensham, M. (1995) *Understanding Primary Science: Ideas, Concepts and Explanations*. London: Paul Chapman.

Wolfendale, S. and Bryans, T. (1983) *Handbook for Teachers: Perceptual Motor Development*. Stafford: National Association for Remedial Education (NARE).

Wood, D. (1988) *How Children Think and Learn*. Oxford: Basil Blackwell.

● ● ● Index

EARLY EXPLORATIONS IN SCIENCE

Jane Johnston

The introduction of the National Curriculum in Science at Key Stage 1 has highlighted the need for a close look at teaching and learning in early years science. Children are immersed in science through their everyday experiences and these early science experiences will shape their future development.

This book explores issues such as the range, nature and importance of pre-school and Key Stage 1 science experiences. It considers the development of scientific skills, conceptual understanding and attitudes in young children, through observation, exploration and creative activities. Throughout there is an attempt to engage the reader in thoughtful consideration of their role in early scientific development and of the important role played by parents and children themselves. The book will be invaluable reading for all trainee and practising primary school teachers.

This book:

- provides several examples of stimulating and creative classroom activities;
- is accessibly written to support teachers and build confidence in teaching primary science;
- is firmly grounded in good early years practice.

Contents
Pre-school science experiences – The importance of exploration in the development of early years science knowledge and skills – Seeking creativity in science activities – Developing positive attitudes in science – Developing the teacher's role – References – Index.

184pp   0 335 19540 7 (Paperback)   0 335 19541 5 (Hardback)

ENRICHING EARLY MATHETMATICAL LEARNING

Grace Cook, Lesley Jones, Cathy Murphy and Gillian Thumpston

This book is a rich resource intended to support practising and trainee teachers with their teaching of mathematics in the early years. It comprises twenty activities which can be used as starting points. For each activity there are suggestions about how children might respond and guidance as to how the children may be further developed as learners. Support is also given to enable the teacher to embed the learning in a theoretical framework and make links with the National Curriculum.

All of the activities have been tried and tested in school and suggestions are made about the way in which these might be integrated into general classroom topics. There is a strong focus on formative assessment and how this can inform future planning.

Special features include:

- very accessible to teachers
- attractive and user-friendly format
- detailed support for introducing and extending activities which cover each area of the National Curriculum
- focus on using and applying maths at the early stages of Key Stage 1.

Contents
Introduction – Activities linked to the National Curriculum Programmes of study – Handfuls – Ladybirds – Rosie the hen – Jumps and hops – Number ladder – Calculator numbers – Higher and lower – Secret number – Feely bag pairs – Boxes – Comparing containers – Towers – Robots – Wrapping paper – Here comes the dustcart – Dolly mixtures – Fabric beanies – What's missing? – Egg boxes – Unifix towers – Appendix – Resources – Bibliography.

104pp   0 335 19666 7 (Paperback)

EDUCATING THE WHOLE CHILD
CROSS-CURRICULAR SKILLS, THEMES AND DIMENSIONS

John and Iram Siraj-Blatchford (eds)

This book approaches the 'delivery' of the cross-curricular skills, themes and dimensions from a perspective emphasizing the culture of primary schools and the social worlds of children. The authors argue that the teaching of skills, attitudes, concepts and knowledge to young children should not be seen as separate or alternative objectives, but rather as complementary and essential elements of the educational process. It is the teacher's role to help children develop and build upon the understandings, skills, knowledge and attitudes which they bring with them into school. Learning for young children is a social activity where new skills and understandings are gained through interaction with both adults and with their peers. Each of the approaches outlined in the book is thus grounded in an essential respect and empathy for children and childhood as a distinct stage in life and not merely a preparation for the world of adulthood. For instance, the authors argue that responsibilities and decision-making are everyday experiences for children and that they need to be able to develop attitudes and skills which enable them to participate fully in their own social world.

Contents
Cross-curricular skills, themes and dimensions: an introduction – Little citizens: helping children to help each other – Effective schooling for all: the 'special educational needs' dimension – Racial equality education: identity, curriculum and pedagogy – 'Girls don't do bricks': gender and sexuality in the primary classroom – Children in an economic world: young children learning in a consumerist and post-industrial society – Catching them young: careers education in the primary years – Understanding environmental education for the primary classroom – Health education in the primary school: back to basics? – The place of PSE in the primary school – Index.

Contributors
John Bennett, Debra Costley, Debbie Epstein, Peter Lang, Val Millman, Lena Patel, Alistair Ross, Ann Sinclair Taylor, Iram Siraj-Blatchford, John Siraj-Blatchford, Balbir Kaur Sohal, Janice Wale.

192pp   0 335 19444 3 (paperback)   0 335 19445 1 (hardback)